MILLION DOLLAR HOLD'EM:
Limit Cash Games

MILLION DOLLAR HOLD'EM:
Limit Cash Games

JOHNNY CHAN
and
MARK KAROWE

CARDOZA PUBLISHING

Cardoza Publishing is the foremost gaming publisher in the world, with a library of over 200 up-to-date and easy-to-read books and strategies. These authoritative works are written by the top experts in their fields and with more than 9,000,000 books in print, represent the best-selling and most popular gaming books anywhere.

FIRST EDITION

Library of Congress Catalog Card No: 2005930778
ISBN: 1-58042-200-4

Visit our web site—www.cardozapub.com—or write for a full list of books and computer strategies.

CARDOZA PUBLISHING
P.O. Box 1500, Cooper Station, New York, NY 10276
Phone (800) 577-WINS
email: cardozapub@aol.com
www.cardozapub.com

ABOUT THE AUTHORS

Johnny Chan has won ten World Series of Poker titles—tied for the most ever with Doyle Brunson. He shot to fame in the late 1980s with the most incredible feat in tournament poker history, winning the main championship event of the World Series of Poker in 1987 *and* 1988 and almost winning an unprecedented third consecutive title in 1989 (he finished in 2nd place to Phil Hellmuth). Chan, who had an unforgettable cameo in the movie, Rounders, in which he is portrayed as the greatest poker player in the world, is one of the all-time legends of the game and one of the very best cash players. He was inducted into the Poker Hall of Fame in 2002.

Mark Karowe is an expert card player who has teamed up with Johnny to write for a number of publications. He is also co-author of *Play Poker Like Johnny Chan - Book One: Getting Started.*

The following is a sampling of some of the higher buy-in titles Johnny holds:

1982 Golden Nugget ½ Hold'em ½ Stud Champion
1982 America's Cup Main Event Champion
1983 Stairway to the Stars No-Limit Hold'em Champion
1985 WSOP Limit Hold'em Champion
1986 Frontier Triple Crown Classic - won three Events
1987 Diamond Jim Brady Main Event Champion
1987 WSOP Main Event Champion
1988 WSOP Main Event Champion
1988 Binion's Hall of Fame Main Event Champion
1989 WSOP Main Event Runner Up
1989 Binion's Hall of Fame Main Event Champion
1991 Bicycle Club Tournament of Champions Winner
1994 Commerce Classic III Deuce-to-Seven Lowball Champion
1994 WSOP Seven Card Stud Champion
1996 Super Bowl of Poker Main Event Champion
1997 WSOP Deuce-to-Seven Draw Champion
2000 WSOP Omaha Pot-Limit Champion
2002 WSOP Match Play No-Limit Hold'em Champion
2003 WSOP No-Limit Hold'em Champion
2003 WSOP Pot-Limit Omaha Champion
2005 WSOP Pot-Limit Hold'em Champion

TABLE OF CONTENTS

SECTION

INTRODUCTION

This book is going to show you how to win money at limit hold'em, poker's most popular cash game. You'll get a rare opportunity to get into the mind of the man who has won an incredible ten World Series of Poker titles—no player in the history of poker has more—as we pick out illustrative hands and show you how we think our way through the betting and the bluffing. You'll learn the thought process behind how a hand is played, the alternative ways it could have been played, and some powerful approaches to making money at limit hold'em cash games.

If you are a winning player and want to make more money, or if you aspire to become a winning player, there is a wealth of practical advice in this book. We have filled the book with tons of example hands for key situations you'll face to illustrate some of the most important concepts used by top limit hold'em players. In many instances, we show the hole cards of opponents so you can get an idea of how some people play hands and so you can see what kind of hands you might be up against.

You'll learn the many different concepts that go into hands you play—aggression, getting maximum value, avoiding traps, not giving free cards, getting free or cheap cards, making extra bets, saving bets, and reading players. We'll also cover concepts like playing defense, bluffing, semi-bluffing, continuation bets, isolating players, making tough laydowns, playing marginal hands, and mixing up your play—powerful ideas which will be a part of many of the hands you'll play.

Some of the example hands are from actual play, while others were created specifically for this book. The limits at which the actual hands were played have been changed to more closely reflect the limits at which the majority of people play. The names of the players have been changed as well. Although we've focused on ring games, many of the examples feature less than a full table, just as you would normally encounter in actual play.

Many of these concepts are not effective in very low-limit games, because the reasoning behind the play of these hands is based on the assumption that many of your opponents are good players and are actively thinking about the hands in which they are involved. The fact is, however, that at very low limits, many players are thinking only about the two cards they hold and not giving much thought to their opponents' cards.

But at games in which your opponents are thinking players, the concepts we cover here should pay you very large dividends indeed.

BECOMING A WORLD CLASS PLAYER

If you wish to become a world-class player, you must constantly assess the different variables that make each hand unique. You should go over each of the situations in the book a number of times to assimilate all of the concepts involved. There is seldom one correct way to play a hand.

It would also be a good idea for you to sit down with this book after your playing sessions, think about the hands you played, and ask yourself which concepts were involved. While the hands that you played will not be exactly like the ones in this book, almost every session will contain a closely related situation. You can increase your understanding of the game by comparing how we recommend playing similar hands to the way that you played yours.

USING MULTIPLE WINNING CONCEPTS

Each section of the book presents a group of hands that illustrate closely related concepts. Since many concepts are involved in the playing of any one hand, you may find the same ideas referred to in several examples. Pay attention to the subtle differences in how the concepts are used according to the differences in the example hands. You should also observe the number of concepts that can be involved in any one hand, and how a single move by one player can make it worthwhile to use a different set of concepts to play the hand more effectively.

LEARN HOW TO MAXIMIZE PROFITS

Limit hold'em is a complicated game whose strategy changes constantly depending on the players involved. You might play in a game one night with a bunch of tight players and another night with some very loose-aggressive players. Strategies that work well in one game may be ineffective in the other.

Part of your job as a skilled player is to determine what kind of game you are in as well as how each opponent in the game plays. That means not only how each player plays in general, but how each player plays as relates to the particular type of game being played. An individual can play very differently based on various factors, including whether he is winning or losing and how the other players are playing. And you should also be aware of how the other players view you. Ask yourself what your table image is and how you can take advantage of it. Do this often. Remember that you can change your current table image over the course of thirty minutes if you decide to.

Part of becoming a world-class player is to develop the ability to "change gears" throughout a session. That ability helps you keep your opponents guessing and allows you to increase the amount of value you can extract from a situation.

Many of the ideas in this book have never appeared in print before. It is certainly to your advantage to be one of the first to understand them all.

SECTION

THE ENVIRONMENT

OVERVIEW

Many different factors go into defining your poker environment. Let's talk about some of them. The first is the physical location of the cardroom. Is it convenient to you? Is it easy for you to get to? When you are deciding which ones to play in, keep in mind that you will be going to these cardrooms over and over again. All of the time that you spend getting to the club is time you aren't playing. Therefore, select rooms located within a reasonable distance of where you live. You may want to devote some time to playing in various poker rooms around the country to figure out where the best games for you are being spread.

MY START

I started out playing in private games around the Houston, Texas, area. When I found myself winning money, I began to take junkets to Las Vegas. On the first several trips, I didn't play poker. I didn't even know there was poker in Las Vegas. I went for the table games, like blackjack and craps. After a number of visits, during which I lost all of my money, I found my way to the Golden Nugget in downtown Las Vegas and to my first Nevada poker game. I began in the $10-$20 game and quickly moved on to no limit, and it didn't take me long to realize that there was a lot more opportunity for me in Las Vegas than there was in Houston.

So there I was living in Houston, while the games I wanted to play in were halfway across the country in Las Vegas. The only logical choice was to relocate to where those games were. A similar thing happened to me 15 or so years later when the Los Angeles-area cardrooms began to offer Nevada-style poker games.

Up until that time, only lowball and draw were played in the California cardrooms. But around 1987 certain changes in legislation allowed California cardrooms to start offering hold'em, seven-card stud, and other popular casino poker games. As any good pro would do, I took a flight to the Los Angeles area to see what was going on. I was amazed and delighted to find a regular $300-$600 hold'em game being played at the Bicycle Club.

A few top Las Vegas pros had already been camping out for a month or so and it became evident to me that this was the place to be playing. I flew back and forth several times over the next couple of months until it became clear that, for a while at least, I would be spending most of my time in Los Angeles. Once I realized that, I started to look around for a house to buy in California.

Two main desires drove the search for my ideal house. The first was to be in a safe, upscale area. The second was that I wanted the location to be convenient to all of the cardrooms where I was likely to be playing. So when I narrowed my possible selection down to a few different houses, I drove to and from the various places where I would be playing. I drove at different times of day and night and tried multiple routes, because I realized that I would do the round trip at least five or six times a week. After a little while, I was able to decide which was the most convenient house among the few that I really liked and I made an offer. I still live there today. Of course, I kept my home in Las Vegas, because I travel regularly between the two cities.

A COMFORTABLE ENVIRONMENT

A big factor in choosing the optimal poker environment is whether you feel comfortable in the cardroom.

Although nowadays the majority of poker rooms are becoming nonsmoking, that wasn't always the case. For many nonsmokers, a room that prohibits smoking might be preferable to one that has somewhat better games but allows smoking.

You should enjoy the company of the people that you'll be playing with. It doesn't make a lot of sense to spend the majority of your time playing in a room where the personalities of most of the people you'll be playing against irritate you. Sometimes it's okay to play in a place like that, if the game is particularly good, but I wouldn't make a regular practice of it. If it was the only place with poker in the area, I would spend some time looking for other locations, even if it meant moving. One of the nice things about playing poker for a living is that you're free to move anywhere you want and start to work the first day you get to your new location. Playing professional poker necessitates spending a great deal of time sitting around with the same group of people. You'll enjoy your life as a player more if you like being with the regulars at the casino you decide to play in.

Also, you want to trust the management of whatever cardrooms you make your home. You don't want to be worrying about whether the game you're playing in is honest. If you have any serious doubts, I highly recommend you look for another place to play. Just the fact that you're wondering whether the game is honest is enough to decrease your edge to the point that you're almost certain to be doing better playing somewhere else. Occasionally you may feel that the management is honest but there are a few players who are not. If you're forced to play with those players on a regular basis, that is another reason to look elsewhere. Happily, in today's games, that type of situation is rare.

The presence of distractions might influence whether you find the environment comfortable. For instance, if you play in a Nevada casino, the cardroom might be right next to a large bank of slot machines. Over time, the noise from the slots can be distracting and irritating. This would be another reason to look for another venue.

Almost all California casinos serve food to the players, and most comp the mid- and high-level players. Even though I like to eat out at restaurants, because I spend so much time at the tables I often order food at the club I'm playing in. If most other things are equal, I prefer to play at the club that offers the best food. It may seem trivial, but day in and day out it sure makes a difference.

Another aspect to consider is the quality of the staff. I want the people who run the board to be very efficient and keep things running smoothly. I'd like the floorpeople to be available and attentive. If any disputes arise, I'd like them to be handled in a quick and efficient manner. The quality of the dealers is especially important to me. I want to know that they are well-trained and able to maintain their focus on the game at all times. We play for a lot of money and we don't want to have a dealer's mistake deciding the outcome of a hand. Quality dealers are helpful to professional players because they keep the game moving along at a good pace, make relatively few errors, and have a professional attitude. If a club fails to train its dealers properly, look for another place to play. And when you find the optimal room, do reward good dealers properly by tipping them appropriately.

Also consider the parking situation. Does the club provide a safe environment for you when you park your car and walk into the club? Is there valet parking and do you feel comfortable using it? If not, is there a safe parking lot adequately staffed with security? Do you feel comfortable getting from your car to the building? These are not trivial matters. All it takes is one bad experience to make playing at a club not worth it. I feel this is fundamentally the club's responsibility, but unfortunately some don't take it very seriously.

Many subtle factors go into deciding whether the environment is a good one for you. Part of your responsibility as a professional player is to weigh the various factors and make the best decision.

GAME SELECTION

Game selection is one of the most important elements that determine your eventual win rate. To select games properly, you have to be able to assess your own skill level accurately. You also need to be able to judge your abilities accurately in relation to the various opponents you will be playing against. Although you may be an excellent player, you nevertheless may not do particularly well against certain opponents, even if they're less competent than you.

Be aware of whom you do well against and whom you have trouble with. It doesn't make a game unplayable to contain one or more opponents that you don't do well against, but it does mean that you should be especially cautious about getting involved with those players. Over time, there is a good chance that if you carefully observe the opponents with whom you have trouble, you may be able to overcome your disadvantage with them. Don't be impatient, though, because to unravel the subtleties of why you do or don't do well may take quite a while.

Often you'll be in a game that is quite good for a while and then certain players quit, and some very tough players take their place. When this happens, it may be time for you to quit if you feel your edge is significantly decreased. There is nothing wrong with leaving a game and finding another elsewhere. Although nowadays I tend to play only for the very highest stakes, which frequently are the toughest games, as I was moving up through the limits, I used to jump around from game to game. In a particular cardroom, if there were a few players whom I felt I had a big advantage over, I would often follow them around from table to table. There's no shame in that. While it's nice to have the macho image gained from playing at the highest levels, it often can be detrimental to your bankroll. Spend the majority of your time playing against players you can beat, especially when you're trying to move up.

Also consider the complete table makeup. A table full of maniacs may not be as profitable as a table with a few maniacs who often play to the end and five rather passive but somewhat tight players. This is because at the second table you will often find yourself in a hand with only one or two players who play very badly. When the entire table likes to play to the end, you are going to have to show down a good hand every time. If you play in games in which you can place yourself in pots that involve just you and one or two relatively unskilled players, you will have many more chances to use the full range of your poker skills.

Don't misinterpret what I'm saying, though, as meaning that you will not make an excellent profit in games in which the majority of the players play terribly. You may hear fairly good players claim that they can't win in games in which everyone likes to call to the end. This is a fallacy. It may seem that way sometimes, because you do have to show down a hand most of the time to win the pot in games like that. This can make the long run a very long time in coming.

The bottom line is that you will make excellent money eventually if you spend a lot of time playing in very loose games, but the ride will be rather rocky. What generally happens in such games is that you have very long break-even periods and then you win a ton of money in a short period of time. Many players get so frustrated with the long break-even periods that they don't give themselves the chance to experience the inevitable rush that more than makes up for all of the breaking even.

As you are building your bankroll, and trying to move up through the limits, selecting the best games to play in is a prime consideration. If you carefully select your games and choose only very good ones to play in, your win rate per hour will be much higher. In addition, your bankroll requirements will be smaller. Therefore, proper game selection will get you where you want to go more quickly with less risk.

If you've been doing very well for a few months, I think it's reasonable to take a shot at some tougher games. Occasionally playing above your head against players you feel you might not be able to beat is, in the long run, a good way to pick up some new tricks and improve your game. I just wouldn't make a habit of it.

SEATING

Picking the best seat in the game is definitely a skill. Of course, you can't always get the best one; often there will be a few pros in the game and they will all be vying for them.

To some extent, your style determines where the best seat for you is. But more often the style and ability of your opponents is the deciding factor. It often pays to try to locate yourself to the left of loose-aggressive players. This is because they play more hands than most of the other players, and they tend to be very aggressive when they do. If you're sitting to their left, you know ahead of time when they are going to be in the hand and you also see if you're facing a raise from them or not. That's not to say that other players may not raise behind you, but loose-aggressive players raise a lot more frequently than the average player.

Ideally, you want to know before you commit your chips if the pot is going to be raised. If you sit in front of the loose-aggressive players, frequently you're not sure whether the pot will be raised, forcing you to pass on many borderline hands. If you're sitting behind the loose-aggressive players, and one of them raises, it's easy to get rid of those hands without committing extra money to them. But when they're out of the hand, you can profitably play some hands you would be better off tossing if they're to your left.

Another reason why it's preferable to sit behind a loose-aggressive player is that it's easier to isolate him. By definition, such a player tends to play more hands than is optimal. For that reason, you'd like to be able to get heads-up with him when you have premium cards. If you sit behind him, when he raises and you have a good hand that plays well against one opponent, you can reraise and frequently knock out all the other players so that you're able to play heads-up against the loose-aggressive player. If you are sitting in front of him, and you raise with good cards, that sometimes signals him that it's best to lay down his. When he does that, you miss the opportunity of playing the best hand against him. Other times, when you raise coming in with a hand that you prefer to play against just one or two opponents, a loose-aggressive player calls your raise, enticing other players to come along as well. This often results in your playing a multiway pot with a holding you prefer to play heads-up.

It's a big advantage to know ahead of time whether the loose-aggressive player, who may play as many as 50 percent more hands than you, is going to be in the pot. The only way to know that is to sit behind him. At the other extreme, it's probably a good idea to sit to the right of tight players. One reason for this is that they play relatively few hands, and when you raise they often fold. They're fairly predictable and it's always nice to have those types of players behind you so that you can more accurately assess the likely progression of the pot.

The more you play, the more you will understand the various subtleties that go into determining which are the best seats for you. I just mentioned two rather broad categories of players, but there are many intricacies in every player's game. To determine the best place for you to sit at the table, get in the habit of taking into account the various aspects of all of your opponents' playing styles and contrast them to your own.

BANKROLL

Your poker bankroll is money that you set aside *specifically* for playing poker. What many aspiring professional players don't understand is that you must keep your playing bankroll completely separate from any money that you use to pay your day-to-day expenses. You don't pay for your rent or mortgage, medical expenses, groceries, auto insurance, school tuition, or vacation expenses out of your poker bankroll. You don't use money from your poker bankroll to pay for drinks on a Saturday night, go out to the movies, buy new clothes, or pay for repairs to your car. The only thing that you can use your poker bankroll for is playing poker.

What that also means is that you should have another way to pay all of the day-to-day expenses. You may really need two or more bankrolls. You need your poker bankroll and then you need a source of funding to pay all of your other expenses. If you happen to have a job at the same time you are playing poker, you may be able to pay all of those expenses out of the income that you derive from your regular job. If you don't have a regular job and poker is your only source of income, then you have to have a nest egg from which you pay all your living expenses.

Eventually, you can take money out of your poker bankroll and add it to your nest egg. One reasonable way to do this is to make a pact with yourself that every time you double a bankroll you will put half of the money you won into a new bankroll and the other half into your nest egg. If you were to follow that particular formula you would be increasing your playing bankroll by 50 percent every time you double it. If you're fortunate enough to have a sufficient nest egg, you may be able to add all of the money that you win to your poker bankroll, which would allow you to move up in stakes that much more quickly.

I'll say it again: keep your playing bankroll separate from the funds used for paying living expenses. The reason I've mentioned this a few times is that many players end up going broke because they don't make enough money to cover their living expenses and eventually completely deplete their playing bankrolls.

Let's talk a little bit about the size of your poker bankroll. Your poker bankroll should be large enough that negative fluctuations don't cause you to go broke. I'm going to simplify things quite a bit just to make this concept clear. Suppose the greatest player in the world is playing against a terrible player. Let's say that this terrible player calls way too much with almost any two cards and that he very rarely folds on the end.

Now let's say we give the greatest player in the world 10 big bets to play with and we give the terrible player 5,000 big bets to play with. Even though the great player would play every hand better than the terrible player, there is an excellent chance that the terrible player would eventually wind up with all the money. That's because 10 big bets is not enough ammunition for the great player to overcome the luck factor involved. Because the great player cannot bluff out the terrible player, he is going to have to win in a showdown to take any pot. He can fold his hand early if he feels certain he is beaten, thereby saving himself some bets, but each time he does that he will have fewer bets to work with than before the hand started. Unless he can win a number of hands in a row, it is going to be impossible for him to build up his bankroll.

Let's suppose instead that we give the greatest player in the world 25 big bets to work with. Unfortunately, that doesn't put him in a much better situation, because 25 bets is still too small an amount to overcome the luck factor.

However, if we give the greatest player in the world 100 big bets to work with, now he has a much better chance of overcoming the luck factor, increasing his bankroll, and eventually winding up with all the money. If he starts with 100 big bets, he can afford to fold a number of times when he believes he has the worst hand, lose a few pots in which he has the best hand until the last card, and eventually get on a streak in which he wins a number of hands and increases his bankroll size to 150 big bets. Then he might have a streak of cards in which he loses 40 big bets followed by another streak in which he wins 70 big bets. That cycle might continue until eventually he winds up with all the money.

The question is, taking into account all the pertinent factors, how many big bets does the great player need to be assured that he will end up with all the money?

This is a very difficult question to answer, mainly because it is difficult to define all the pertinent factors. Using statistics allows you to figure out a certain player's chance of going broke if you know the bet size, the player's expected win rate, and the player's standard deviation (see glossary), but arriving at the correct answer actually requires a lot more information than that. Again, I am going to simplify things to try to answer the question. First, we'll assume that the poker bankroll is kept separate and used only for playing poker. We'll also assume that your expectancy is more than one big bet per hour and that your standard deviation is about 10 big bets per hour.

One widely accepted theory is that you are quite safe if you have a bankroll of 300 big bets. The problem with this theory is that so many of the important factors vary significantly from player to player. Some of those significant factors are how consistent your play is, how consistent the play of your opponents is, how accurate your assessment of your win rate and standard deviation are, what chance of going broke you are comfortable with, and how closely you follow the requirements necessary to make 300 big bets a valid figure.

A serious player should have a poker bankroll much larger than 300 big bets. I think that for whatever limit you are playing, you need to have at least 500 big bets. That is, you ought to have $10,000 to play $10-$20 limit poker, $15,000 for $15-$30 limit poker, and $30,000 for $30-$60 limit poker. I even go a step further and say that it would not be a bad idea to have *more* than 500 big bets at limits above \$30-\$60. That's because the players are better and thus your overall edge decreases. In addition, your opponents are generally more aggressive at the higher limits, which causes more fluctuation and therefore requires more bankroll.

MOVING UP AND DOWN IN LIMITS

If you are going to make it as a professional player, unless you have unlimited funds, you must start at a certain limit and eventually move up from there. In the very beginning, it makes sense to start at a very low limit. If you are just starting out, we strongly recommend that you read our first book *Play Poker Like Johnny Chan: Book One - Getting Started*. There is nothing wrong with playing small limits until you become accustomed to the environment and to the game. And even if you play reasonably high limits at one particular game, if you're starting to learn a new one it makes a lot of sense to drop down to a much lower limit while learning. Once you start to show a profit at the small limit, it's a good idea to move up a little bit and see how you do.

If you find you don't beat the next level, I recommend that you either drop back down and win some more money, or, at the very least, not move up to another level until you can beat the one you are currently playing. One thing to keep in mind is that you probably have to play at least \$3-\$6 limit to be able to overcome the rake. If you are playing below \$3-\$6 limit, consider it practice and wait until you get up to \$3-\$6 before you expect to show a long-term profit.

Something not mentioned very often is to force yourself to move up in limits if your intention is to become a career player. While there's nothing wrong with staying at a particular limit until you double a couple of bankrolls, I think many players tend to get comfortable at a certain level and never move beyond that. If you find yourself unsatisfied with the amount of money that you're making, the best solution is to learn to beat higher limits and progressively move up over time. On the other hand, if you try a higher limit and continue to feel uncomfortable playing it, it's a good sign that you may not yet be ready for it.

I recommend you try to move up on a regular basis, but if the fluctuations are too stressful for you, it's a good sign that you are playing over your head. If after a few weeks or months, the stress of playing higher does not subside—or you find that you are losing money—it may be best for you to drop down a limit or two. The key is to find a limit that provides you with a win rate that meets your needs and expectations.

Now, let's talk about how you might accomplish moving up. Suppose you start with a suggested 500-big-bet poker bankroll that you use only for playing poker. Suppose also that you have a completely separate funding source for paying all of your living expenses. Let's say you're starting out at $5-$10 limit and you have a $5,000 poker bankroll.

If you have the records to indicate that you are a winning player who wins at a rate of one big bet per hour or higher, consider playing at the $5-$10 level until your bankroll either reaches $10,000 or drops down to $3,000. If you get unlucky and it drops down to $3,000, stop playing at the $5-$10 level and begin playing at the $3-$6 level. If, instead, you do well and increase your bankroll to $10,000, step up to the $10-$20 level. At this point, your main game should be the $10-$20, but you should also feel free to play any smaller limit if the $10-$20 games do not seem worthwhile on a particular day.

If your bankroll then drops back to $5,000, return to the $5-$10 limit games and do not play at the $10-$20 limit until you get your bankroll back up to $10,000. Once you are able to get your bankroll up to $15,000, step up to the $15-$30 limit games. At that point, $15-$30 should be your main game but you should be willing to play $10-$20 and occasionally even smaller games if there is nothing worthwhile at the $15-$30 limit. Again, if you get unlucky and your bankroll drops back to $10,000, no longer play in the $15-$30 games, but make $10-$20 your main limit. However, once you build your bankroll to $30,000, move up to the $30-$60 games.

You can apply this formula for any limit, including $20-$40, $50-$100, $75-$150, $100-$200, and higher limits. The only thing to keep in mind is that the higher you play, the larger the number of big bets you should have in your poker bankroll. This means you might want to wait until you have 1,200 or even 1,500 big bets in your bankroll to play $100-$200 or higher. This is especially true if you intend to play in short-handed games.

At higher limits, the players are tougher and much more aggressive. That means your edge will be smaller and your variance will be greater. Yes, that means a poker bankroll of $300,000 or more for short-handed $100-$200. If, at some point you reach a level at which you are simply unable to show a profit even after hundreds of hours of play, you might consider that the skill level required to beat that limit is simply beyond your capabilities.

If you find such a limit, you can make a decision whether you want to try to improve your game enough that you can beat that limit or whether you would prefer to just earn as much as possible at a lower limit.

Notice that by following this formula, anytime you have a significant series of losses you will readjust your poker bankroll size to contain the required 500 big bets. Using a formula like this, you should be able to occasionally take shots in higher games without jeopardizing your bankroll too much. If you want to be on the safe side, you might consider only taking those shots when your bankroll is above the required 500 big bets for what you have made your regular limit. For instance, let's say you have $12,000 and $10-$20 is your main limit. If you see an especially juicy $15-$30 or $20-$40 game, you might consider risking $1,000 or $2,000 in it. If you lose that money, you should then stick to the $10-$20 games at least until you make another $2,000. Taking the occasional extra risk applies only for especially juicy $15-$30 or $20-$40 games. Normally you would stick to the $10-$20 games until you reached $15,000.

If you're extremely comfortable with a much higher risk level, you may want to try the same formula but instead substitute 300 big bets for the 500-big-bet bankroll size. One of the most important aspects of moving up successfully and yet maintaining a reasonable level of risk is to be willing to drop down in limit after substantial losses.

You also must consider what to do if you need to withdraw money from your poker bankroll for various reasons. You can feel free to do so by sticking to the above formula and just assuming that any withdrawal plays the same role as a loss would. Just remember that when you do withdraw money from your poker bankroll, it is going to postpone your ability to move up in limits and therefore probably cost you some expectancy.

DEVELOPING A STYLE

If you are going to play a lot of poker, you must develop a style that suits you. People's personalities are very different from one another. Similarly, players' styles vary greatly. Some people are very conservative and feel comfortable getting involved in a pot only when they have a very good starting hand. They tend to bet when they have a strong hand and check when they don't. If somebody bets against them and they don't have a strong hand, they usually fold.

Some are a bit more aggressive and feel comfortable getting involved with mediocre hands more often. They also sometimes bet with hands they think may not be the best. When somebody bets at them and they don't have a particularly strong hand, instead of folding they may raise.

Still others are extremely aggressive. They feel comfortable getting involved with almost any two cards if they believe the situation is right. They might raise or reraise with hands with which a tight player might not even call the minimum bet. Superaggressive players are also likely to make any sort of play at any time during the hand, including raising or check-raising on the end after they've missed their draw.

And there is a whole range of playing styles spread between the ones I just mentioned. Also, various players can exhibit different aspects of each style, depending on the circumstances.

The trick for you is to experiment with all the different styles that you believe might suit you and find out which ones you are most comfortable with. This is a long process that should continue throughout your entire career. Although you will eventually settle on a basic style that is best for you most of the time, you should be able to switch styles, at least to some extent, depending upon the situation.

PATTERNS AND TELLS

I think tells are overrated. Occasionally you can catch tells on some players, but the majority of players are pretty good at keeping their tells to a minimum, particularly in limit games, in which the bet sizes are relatively constant. For a good treatment of the subject of tells, I suggest you read *Caro's Book of Poker Tells* by Mike Caro.

I prefer to try to recognize betting patterns. Many players fall into the same patterns over time. They tend to make the same moves in similar situations time and time again, and, if you pay close attention, you can begin to recognize the patterns. For example, many players routinely raise from late position whenever they flop a draw. If you are playing against a player who makes a habit of this, you should often reraise him when you think he's on a draw, and then bet out on the turn if you feel you still have the best hand. That way you make his attempt to save a half a bet cost him an extra bet instead.

Some may routinely check the flop after raising with high cards if they don't make a pair. Players like that are essentially telling you what their hand is. You don't need to have a made hand to win the pot from them. Just bet into them when small cards flop and see what they do. If they raise you, it's safe to assume they have you beat. If you decide to check to them and they check behind you, see what comes on the turn. If it appears to be a card that would not have helped them, bet regardless of what two cards you hold and you will likely win the pot. And if you have a monster, you might want to check and let them catch up so that you can make a little more on the hand.

Some players are so rigid in their hand selection that you can often figure out what they have just by their position and whether they called or raised. For instance, some players play only aces, kings, queens, and A-K under the gun. This makes it very easy for you to make the correct decision about which hands to play and how to play them when they come in under the gun.

There are players who check the flop after raising only when they have a high pair or make a strong hand and bet the flop after raising anytime they miss their hand. For instance, when they raise with A-K, they check anytime they hit an ace or a king, hoping either for a check-raise or to make two bets on the turn, but always bet if the flop comes low cards or otherwise misses their hand.

Some players have the impression that flopping a draw in early position is a license to steal the pot and are extremely aggressive anytime they do. That type of player may also routinely pay a small bet on the flop hoping to catch a backdoor draw on the turn so that he can check-raise you in an attempt to make you lay your hand down. If you come across a player like that, just reraise him when he check-raises you on the turn after a draw has developed.

There are players who never raise you with top pair unless they have an ace or a king kicker, but call you down all the way. If you check to them, they bet top pair. Against that type of player, you may want to bet once, but if you get called you may want to check the turn to him and see what he does. If he bets, you can safely assume that second pair is no good.

Then there are calling stations. They continue to call if they have any chance to win the pot, but bet only with very strong hands. If you have a reasonable hand, you should get as much value as possible against this kind of player. Try not to miss any bets if you feel you are probably ahead. But if this player bets at you, it is time to fold unless your hand is very strong.

You should also be aware that some players routinely call the flop with second or third pair, but fold to a bet on the turn if they fail to make two pair or trips. Against this type of player, you can safely bet the turn and win most of the time. If you get raised, you can assume he has at least two pair.

Many players read a lot of books and develop what is called an "ABC" style of play. That means they play strictly by the book and with very little imagination. Provided you are familiar with what the mainstream books are suggesting they do, you can often be very accurate in assessing what cards they hold.

Personally, I find it much easier to recognize patterns of play than tells. I think the majority of players fall into recognizable patterns that end up being more reliable than tells. After reading this discussion, you probably understand why you must learn to mix up your own play and always keep opponents guessing.

PLAYING YOUR "A" GAME

One of the top elements of success is to play your best game at all times. This means that you must play to the best of your ability during the entire time you're sitting at the table. For many players, this is a difficult task. Since I usually play at the highest limits in the world, a lot of times the only edge I have is when one or more of my opponents is not playing to the best of their abilities. In the very high games the players are so good that when they're all playing at their best there is very little that separates them.

Train yourself to recognize when you start to play in such a way that your edge against your opponents starts to decrease. Ideally, strive to play at the top of your game at all times. Realistically, this is nearly impossible. What is not impossible, though, is to play at 90 to 95 percent of your ability anytime you're sitting at the table. If the level of your play drops below this percentage, be prepared to quit unless the game is absolutely fantastic. If I had to pick the three top elements to help you build your bankroll quickly and easily, I would say they are:

1. Game selection
2. Bankroll management
3. Playing to the best of your ability at all times

GETTING EXERCISE

Many of the top players consider exercise to be an important aspect of their routine. I suggest you do the same. Try to get into the habit of including some cardiovascular exercise in your weekly routine. I recommend four to six days of cardio per week. Although 20 minutes is probably enough, more would be better. Cardiovascular exercise like running or stair climbing or something similar is an excellent way to relieve overall stress and keep you feeling fresh. Maintaining a regular exercise regimen is one of the best ways to make sure that you are prepared for the excessive stress involved in playing poker professionally.

TAKING VACATIONS

It really doesn't matter what type of a profession you have, taking vacations is a crucial element of having a balanced and happy life. For professional poker players, taking vacations is even more important. Playing poker on a daily basis with the intention of deriving your income from it is one of the more stressful jobs you can have. It is also the type of job that is very easy to get burned out at.

Regardless of how great a player you are, you will encounter many, many bad beats and extended losing streaks. Any losing streak is unpleasant, but the longer it goes on, the more stressful it becomes. And even if you have an extended winning streak, the work is very difficult and eventually you will start to get burned out. For these reasons, it is essential that you take an adequate number of vacations.

There are various ways to do this. For many players, the best way is to schedule vacations ahead of time and make sure that they go on them when the time comes. I suggest you do this because far too many players hit a losing streak and eventually start to get burned out. They decide that they need time off, but delay their vacation until they get back to their previous high point.

The big problem with this approach is that sometimes it can take hundreds of hours of play to get back to your previous high point. Also, if you decide that you are burned out because of an extended losing streak, your daily stress level has probably increased significantly. The time to go on vacation is when you decide that you are burned out, not after you win all your money back.

If, instead, you try to win your money back before going on vacation, you'll find yourself playing under great pressure. The quality of your play will almost certainly be lower than when you are feeling refreshed. Also, the playing time will be much more difficult and stressful than when you are rested. In extreme cases, the quality of your play might even drop below winning level, in which case you could be spinning your wheels indefinitely.

If you are one of those rare players who is so in touch with himself that he knows exactly when it is appropriate to go on vacation, you can probably get away without scheduling vacations and just go when you feel it is right to do so. Regardless of how you accomplish it, make sure that you are always in as refreshed a state as possible when you are playing.

HOME LIFE AND FAMILY SUPPORT

Playing a lot of poker is a mixed bag with respect to your personal life. One benefit is that you will probably be a lot more flexible about when you can set time aside to spend with your family and friends. This is both on a day by day basis and in terms of when you may be able to take a few days to a week off. For instance, let's say your daughter has a big soccer game on Wednesday afternoon; it shouldn't be very difficult for you to take that time off to see her game. Or let's say some friends ask you to join them for a golf game in the middle of the week or perhaps go out on a boat on Friday afternoon; that also shouldn't be very difficult for you to fit in. Perhaps your wife or girlfriend really wants to go on vacation in five weeks; you won't have to go through any particular arrangements at work to make that possible.

In other words, you're the boss and there's nobody to answer to when you decide that you would like to take some time off.

On the other hand, sometimes the games are extremely good just when family members or friends would like to have you spending time with them. For instance, on the weekends or when there is a tournament in town you might feel obligated to be playing as opposed to spending time relaxing. You also may be the type of player who likes to play for many days in a row until you start to feel burned out and then you like to take some time off. That sort of schedule might not coincide well with other people's plans.

One disadvantage to playing a lot of poker is that it can be stressful, and your loved ones might not fully appreciate that. They might consider you to be far too moody at times, and you in turn may not feel you're getting the appropriate amount of sympathy and support from them. Also, many times you will end up playing very long hours, sometimes all through the night. You may find yourself coming home at 4 or 5 a.m. and sleeping until noon. It takes a special spouse to feel comfortable with that sort of behavior.

Do keep the lines of communication open so that everybody feels comfortable with the way things are going. If your spouse is not happy with the hours that you keep, the two of you need to discuss that and come to some sort of common ground. If your spouse, children, or friends feel that you are too irritable or moody, you should discuss that with them as well. Because of the stress involved in playing a lot of cards, it's difficult not to be irritable at times, and your friends and family need to understand that and give you a little bit of slack. Nonetheless, you have to understand that nobody likes to be around somebody who is in a bad mood, so you must try to do what you can to be a pleasant person to live with.

The better the communication, the better the chance that you will have a happy home life. If you find yourself in the unfortunate situation in which you are living with people who really don't support what you're doing, you'll have to make some difficult choices. Particularly when you are younger and dating, or have a steady girlfriend or boyfriend, you'll have to make difficult decisions about whether he or she is the right person for you if you're going to be playing a lot of poker. It takes a unique spouse to put up with all the special circumstances surrounding playing poker as a career.

If you feel certain that poker is the profession for you, try to meet someone whose personality is conducive to your lifestyle and profession. On the other hand, if you are really in love with somebody who is uncomfortable with your playing a lot of cards, you may decide that poker full time is not the best way to go.

SECTION

$10-$20 HOLD'EM: NINE-HANDED

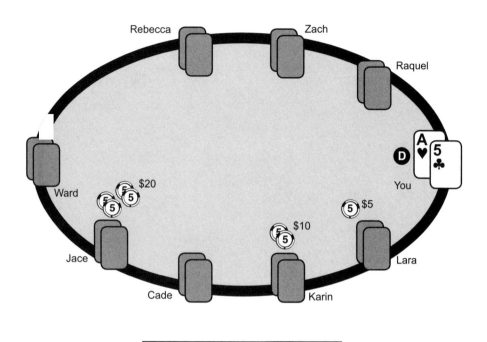

KEY CONCEPTS

• Folding a trap hand when the pot has been raised

You have ace-small offsuit on the button and an early-position player has raised the pot. Everyone has folded to you and you have to make a decision.

There's simply no reason to play this hand, because it's way too easy to be dominated by a better ace or be up against a pair and not know where you stand. Even if the raiser has something like K-Q, he's still probably going to win the pot from you unless you flop an ace. When you do flop an ace, you won't know where you're at and many times you'll either fold the best hand or call all the way with the worst hand.

The best play is to fold the hand before you get in trouble.

$10-$20 HOLD'EM: TEN-HANDED

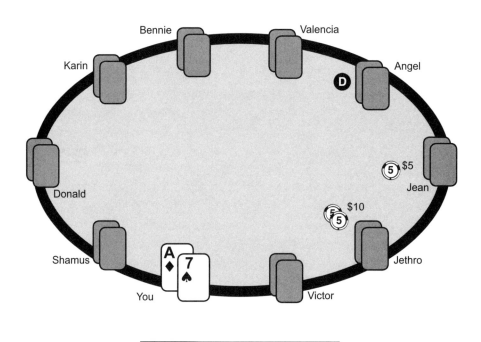

• Folding a trap hand in early position

This hand is fairly straightforward, but I want to show it to you so that you understand that you should not be playing hands like this in early position. You're dealt A-7 offsuit in position No. 4.

There's nothing to think about here. Every time you're in a full game and you get that hand in early position, fold.

$10-$20 HOLD'EM: TEN-HANDED

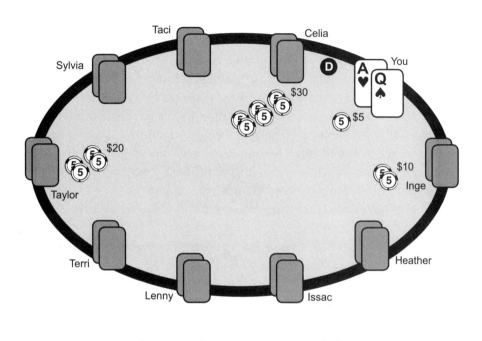

![KEY CONCEPTS]

KEY CONCEPTS

• Folding a trap hand before the flop

You're in the small blind with A-Q offsuit. This is normally an excellent hand. The first four players fold and a middle-position player raises. The next two players fold and the button makes it three bets. You know that these are fairly tight, strong players.

At this point, you have to think about what hands you're likely to be up against. There's a pretty good chance that one of the players has A-K, pocket aces, pocket kings, or pocket queens. Either that, or at least one of the players has a middle pocket pair or better. There's also the possibility that one of the players has the same hand you do. And, finally, you might have the best hand.

You're going to be in the worst position for the entire hand. It's likely that, if you are not beaten already, some of the cards that you need to complete your hand are in the other players' hands. Even if you flop an ace or a queen, you're not going to know where you stand in the hand. If you do hit your hand and it turns out to be the best, it's unlikely that you'll be getting maximum value out of it. These are solid, strong players who have position on you, so, if they are beaten, they will probably either fold or give you minimum action. If you have the best hand and everyone misses, since you are first to act, you will often be outplayed and end up folding. If you do catch an ace or a queen and it's not the best, your opponents will probably extract one or more extra bets from you.

You have hardly anything invested here, so it's a fairly easy fold.

Keep in mind that if you knew the two other players to be loose-aggressive players, you would play.

$10-$20 HOLD'EM: TEN-HANDED

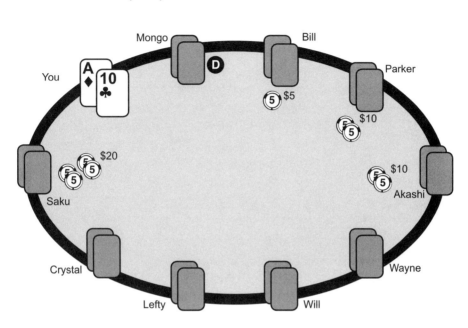

![KEY CONCEPTS]

KEY CONCEPTS

• Folding a trap hand in late position

You're in the cutoff with A♦ 10 ♣ and there's an early-position limper and a late-position raiser before you.

This is a borderline situation. Take into account how your opponents play in this situation. If either has an ace in his hand, it would almost surely be A-10 or better. There's a good chance that at least one of them has a pair. Even if an ace or 10 flops, you're not going to be sure where you stand. Also, if you call, there's a good chance that the size of the pot will attract one or two other players. Your hand doesn't play well in a multiway pot, and yet it's not strong enough to reraise in an effort to narrow the field. That makes this a borderline situation. Your best play is to fold.

45

$10-$20 HOLD'EM: TEN-HANDED

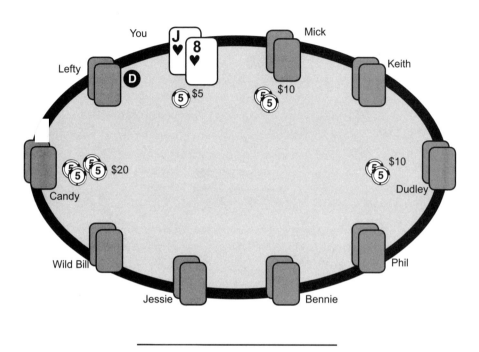

KEY CONCEPTS

• Folding a trap hand preflop to a raise from steal position

You have J-8 suited in the small blind. Position No. 4 limps and the cutoff raises. Here's a hand that looks good, but when you take the time to analyze it, you will find a lot of reasons to pass. First, there is an early-position caller who may well have you dominated with a hand like K-J, Q-J, or J-10. Next, you have to call a raise and will be in the worst possible position for the entire hand. If you were behind the raiser and on or in front of the button, you would fold the hand, so don't be enticed now by your having 25 percent of the call price in already.

One way to help you decide whether to call raises from the

small blind is to ask yourself if you would call the entire raise if you were behind the raiser and either on or before the button. If your answer is no, then you have a clear fold.

If you were playing in a game that had a two-three chip blind structure like the $15-$30 game, you would have a borderline hand and you would have to weigh some of the other factors more heavily.

If you were in the big blind, you would certainly call the raise.

$10-$20 HOLD'EM: NINE-HANDED

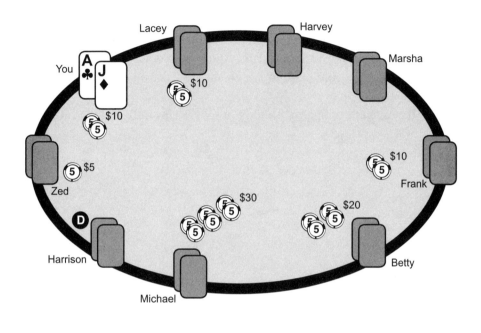

• Playing A-J offsuit in the big blind against two raises

You have A-J in the big blind. The player under the gun limps in and the next few players fold. The player in position No. 7 raises, the cutoff reraises, the button folds, the small blind folds, and it's up to you.

Let's think about the situation. There's an under-the-gun limper. That player probably has a hand like A-J, A-10, A-x suited, K-Q, K-J, or a medium pair. Next there is a middle-position raiser who knows that there is an under-the-gun limper. There is a good chance that player has either a high pair or a hand like A-K, A-Q, or A-J suited. Next the cutoff reraises. That player is likely to have the same type of hand.

Now the question is, do you want to put in two more bets with your cards against the hands your opponents are likely to be playing? This is an easy fold.

$10-$20 HOLD'EM: TEN-HANDED

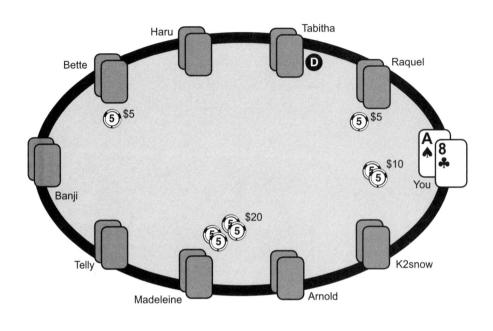

KEY CONCEPTS

• Problems playing ace-small in the big blind against a raise

You are in the big blind with A-8 offsuit. Someone raises from early position and everybody folds around to you. Frankly, most of the time you'd be better off to fold this hand, but in this situation you decide to play, partially because of the extra small blind chip in the pot.

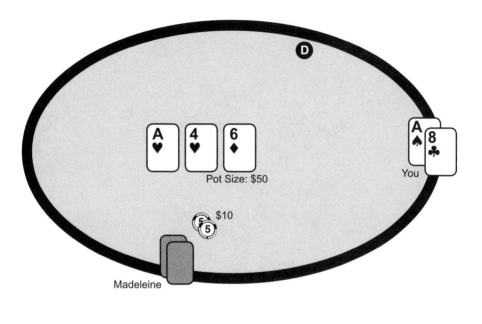

The flop comes A♥ 4♥ 6♦. An ace flopped, but you don't really know where you're at. If you do have the best hand, you'll probably make as much by checking as by betting. You check, your opponent bets, and you call.

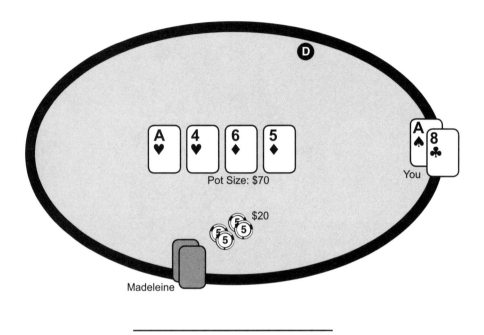

Pot Size: $70

You

$20

Madeleine

The 5♦ that comes on the turn is unlikely to have helped your opponent since she raised coming in from early position. Madeleine is most likely to have a pocket pair, a decent ace, or two face cards. It would not be a particularly bad play to bet out here, because most opponents won't raise you unless they have two pair or better. You decide to check, because if you currently have the best hand, it is probably not too dangerous to give a free card since your opponent is either drawing dead if she has a hand like K-Q or drawing to two cards if she has a pocket pair. There is always the possibility that your opponent now has a flush draw, but it's not too likely.

Your opponent bets and you call.

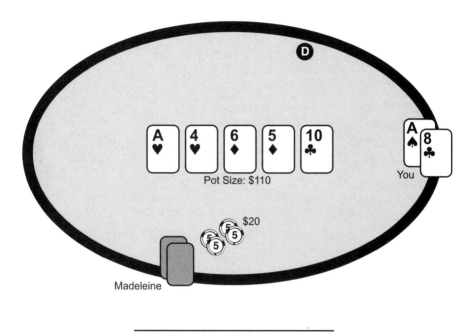

On the end comes the 10♣, a relative blank. You check, hoping to induce a bluff from a busted hand. If your opponent has a better ace than you, she will be betting anyway, so you will lose the same amount as if you bet and she calls. There is no sense trying to knock Madeleine off a better hand by betting, because she certainly will call with any hand that could beat yours.

You could also bet out, attempting to get another bet out of the holder of a hand that might otherwise check the river. If you know your opponent to be the type of player who would not bet anything less than a strong ace in this spot, that would be the best play. If you did bet out and were raised, you should probably fold.

You check and Madeleine bets.

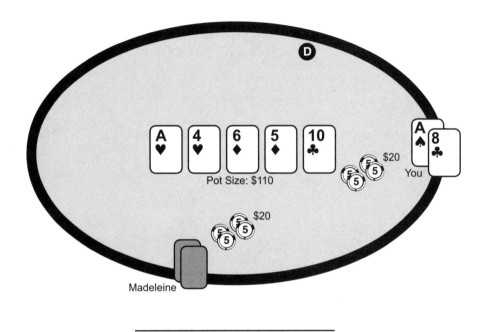

There is nothing to do here but call. On this particular hand, you got lucky because your opponent bet an inferior hand all the way through either because she thought it was the best hand or because she hoped you would fold a bad ace. But you can see the difficulty with calling a bet from early position with a hand like A-8 offsuit. You just never know where you're at. Much of the time, you would be against a better ace and end up just calling off your money. Other times, you would have the best hand but your opponent would check on the turn and fold on the end if you bet, so you wouldn't make much money.

$10-$20 HOLD'EM: EIGHT-HANDED

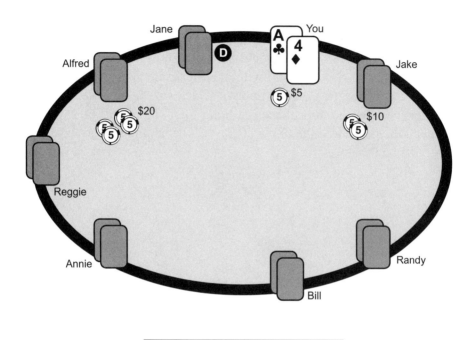

KEY CONCEPTS

• Playing ace-small to a raise from steal position

Here is a situation that comes up often. You have ace-small unsuited in the small blind. Everybody folds to a late-position player, and he raises. Much of the time, you should fold your hand here. If you know the player to be the sort who would often have an inferior hand, you can consider reraising and taking the lead on the flop; you may be able to win the pot that way. Many times, though, you will find yourself up against a better hand, especially in games in which players are playing premium hands. Even if you reraise with the best hand, you will often get outplayed if you miss the flop.

If you had A-8, A-9, or better, you would be a lot more inclined to reraise and play it for the best hand.

The advantage of reraising over calling is that you can often make the big blind fold, thereby getting some dead money into the pot. If you do reraise, you should be prepared to bet both the flop and the turn, as most players will take a card off regardless when they are getting 8 to 1 on their money, which will be the case if you reraise and bet the flop. If the big blind folds, there will be seven bets in the pot before the flop and you will be adding another when you bet on the flop.

SECTION

4

OVERVIEW

Playing hands well from the blinds can be quite difficult. Although you already have some money involved, you'll be in the worst or second-worst position throughout the entire hand. Even so, there are a few things you can take advantage of just because you are the first or second to act. One of the most important is that you have the first opportunity to bluff. Closely related is that a lot of players will give you credit for hitting rag cards if they flop. Some of the examples in this section deal with those ideas.

The discussion also addresses the differences between playing a one-two blind structure and a two-three blind structure. The $10-$20 game with blinds of $5 and $10 is a one-two structure, while the $15-$30 game with blinds of $10 and $15 is a two-three structure. The primary difference is that, because you are getting much better odds in the latter structure, you have to be a lot more liberal with your preflop calls from the small blind. In fact, in an unraised pot in the two-three blind structure game, very few, if any, hands are unplayable preflop from the small blind.

The other major difference is that a larger percentage of the pots are multiway in the two-three structure games. This is because the small blind does call more frequently than in the one-two structure which has a domino effect. Because other players expect multiway pots, they tend to call more liberally as well.

In addition, this section discusses betting when you have no other way to win. Many times you know you can't win by checking the hand down or by checking on the river. In some of those situations, particularly when you believe your opponents are weak, it's a good idea to bet in an attempt to induce the other players to fold. This is more effective against only one opponent, but can also work against multiple opponents. It's often more effective to try this from early rather than late position, because, since no one has yet checked, you have a bit more credibility.

$10-$20 HOLD'EM: NINE-HANDED

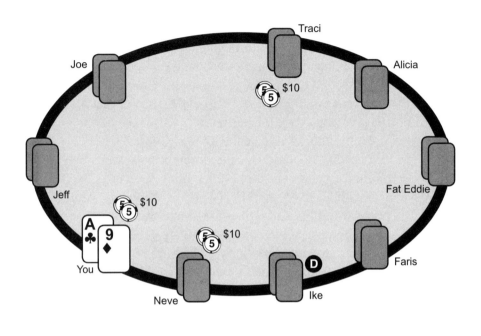

KEY CONCEPTS

• The first bet often wins the pot

In this hand, you have A-9 offsuit in the big blind. One player in middle position has limped in and the small blind has called.

You check.

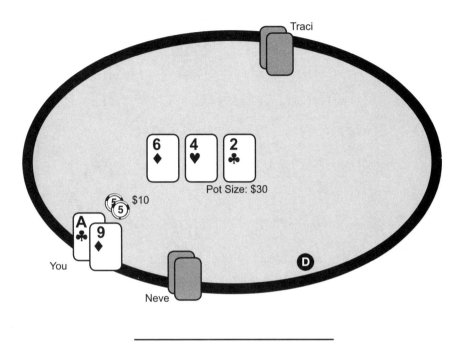

The flop comes 6-4-2 rainbow and the small blind checks to you. These cards are unlikely to have helped the middle-position player. The most likely hand for that player to have is something like J-10, Q-10, K-10, Q-J, or perhaps a small-to-middle pair. When rags like this flop, it's easy for other players to believe that the cards may have hit one or both of the blinds. Unless the middle-position player has a pocket pair, there is a very good chance that you have the best hand. The small blind has checked indicating that she probably doesn't have a piece of this board. The middle-position player probably has two medium overcards to this board, so you decide your best chance to win the hand is to bet right out.

If you bet, you have a decent chance to win the pot.

$10-$20 HOLD'EM: FIVE-HANDED

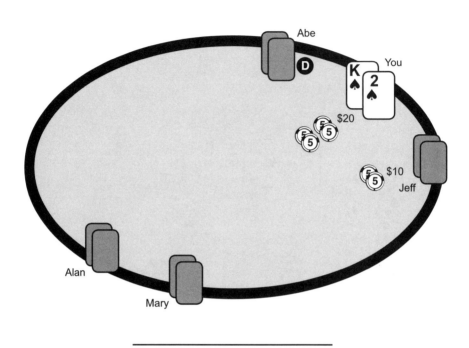

KEY CONCEPTS

• First position blind play: betting when you would call anyway

You are in the small blind and everyone folds to you. You have K♠ 2♠, a better-than-average hand. In this situation, you should usually raise, hoping to win the blinds. If you get called, you still have a playable hand. Be the aggressor in these situations, because often neither of you will hit the flop.

You raise and your opponent calls, which is usually the case in a small-vs.-big-blind heads-up situation. Most players will not fold the big-blind when the small blind raises, because they are getting 3 to 1 odds and have position.

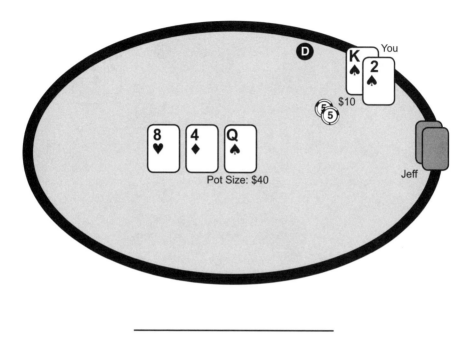

The flop, 8♥ 4♦ Q♠, has missed you completely, but you may still have the best hand. You've shown initial strength and it is not likely to be a great flop for your opponent either. You bet.

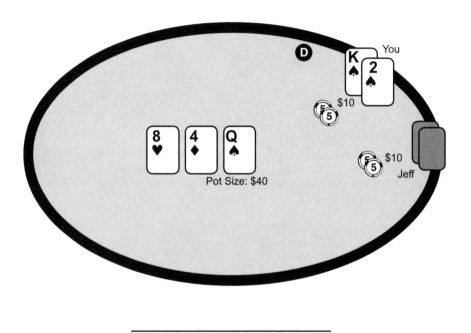

Your opponent calls. That is not the result you wanted, but you can pick up a flush draw or a king on the turn. You'll decide what to do according to what comes on the turn.

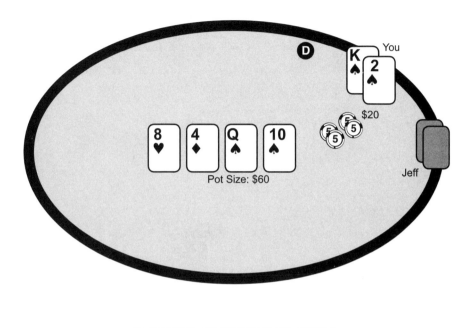

The 10♠ comes, giving you a flush draw with one overcard, for 12 likely wins if you are not ahead already. Since you are going to call anyway, you continue betting.

You bet and you opponent folds.

If the turn card had been a complete blank, you would use your knowledge of your opponent to determine whether or not he is on a draw. If you thought he was, you would probably continue betting and try to take the pot on the end if you thought he missed. If you thought he had a piece of the board, you'd likely check the turn and fold if he bet.

$15-$30 HOLD'EM: TEN-HANDED

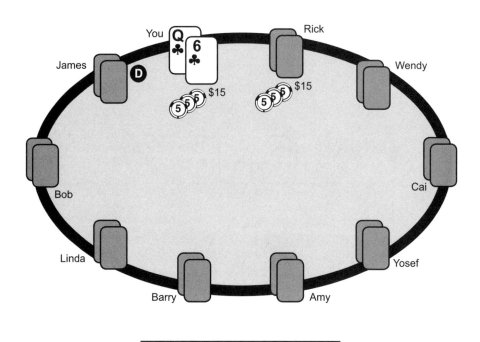

KEY CONCEPTS

• Playing the player: the first bet often wins the pot

You have Q♣ 6♣ in the small blind and everyone folds to you. You can play this situation two ways, and they largely depend on who your opponent is and what your image is. If there is a decent chance your opponent will fold if you raise, you should usually do so and try to win the pot right there. If you think he won't fold, then raise only with the stronger hands, and otherwise just call. There is no reason to get extra money involved in poor position with an average hand unless putting more money in will help you win the pot. Folding is rarely an option with the two-three chip blind structure of this $15-$30 game, because you are getting 5 to 1 odds on your call.

Since you have just a slightly above-average hand and you don't think your opponent will fold if you raise, you just call. Your opponent checks behind you.

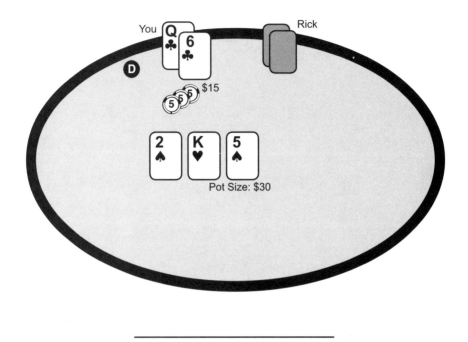

The flop comes 2♠ K♥ 5♠. When you get a flop like this in an unraised heads-up pot, it's quite likely that it has not given your opponent a strong hand. Since he didn't raise before the flop, he likely does not have an ace or a pocket pair. Unless he has a 2, a 5, a king, 3-4, or a spade draw, he's probably missed the flop completely. It's a good idea to bet and try to win the pot. If betting out wins slightly less than one out of two times, you make a profit because you will sometimes win later in the hand even if you get called. If you do get called and don't hit a 6 or a queen, then try to show it down unless you make a hand on the river. That is, check and hope your opponent also checks.

So, bet out because your opponent will fold often enough to make it a profitable play.

$10-$20 HOLD'EM: TEN-HANDED

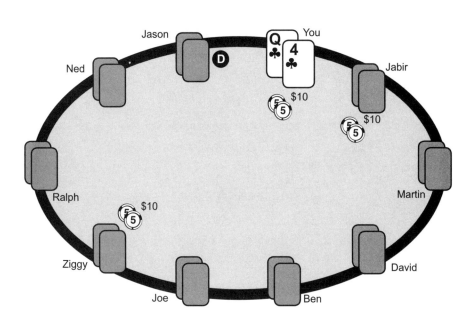

KEY CONCEPTS

- Playing a mediocre hand from the small blind
- Semibluffing at a rag flop from the small blind
- Betting when you would call anyway

The player in position No. 7 limps. Everyone else folds. You have suited queen-small (Q♣ 4♣). This is a clear call because you are getting 5 to 1 on your money and you have a slightly above-average suited hand. The big blind checks.

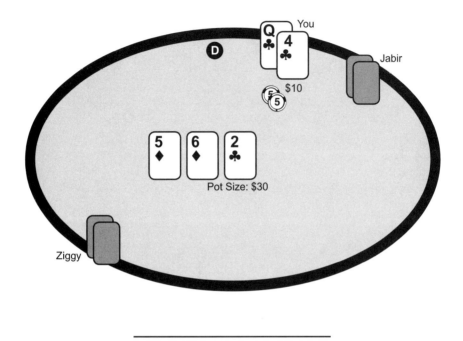

The flop comes 5♦ 6♦ 2♣. When no one has shown strength, the first bet can often win the pot. When small cards flop, you have a slight steal advantage over middle- or late-position callers because it is more likely those cards will have hit your hand than theirs. You should often try betting out to see if you can win the pot without a contest. In a spot like this, where you are going to call anyway, it makes perfect sense to bet out. Also, since no one has raised before the flop, the pot size is rather small and less attractive to anyone who does not have a made hand.

You bet and win a small pot. Had you been called, however, you still had a few ways to win the pot. You might pair your queen and win, you might hit the inside straight, or you might backdoor a flush.

$15-$30 HOLD'EM: TEN-HANDED

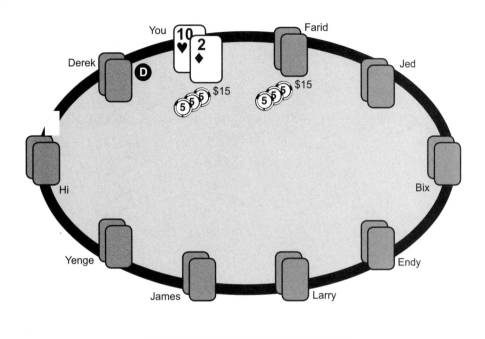

KEY CONCEPTS

• Betting when you have no other way to win
• The first bet often wins the pot

This example is for a game with a two to three blind structure. As mentioned earlier, in games with this blind structure you need to be more liberal calling from the small blind because you are getting much better odds than in a one to two blind structure. For instance, in a $15-$30 game, the blinds are $10 and $15 and it costs only $5 to limp. You are getting 5 to 1 odds to call against only the big blind when everybody has folded to you and you are in the small blind. In a $10-$20 game, since the blinds are $5 and $10, you are only getting 3 to 1 in the same spot.

Here everybody has folded to you in the small blind and you have a trash hand (10♥ 2♦), but because you are getting 5 to 1 odds, you can call with any two cards. The only time you wouldn't call with substandard cards would be if the big blind always raises when you limp from the small blind. You call and the big blind checks.

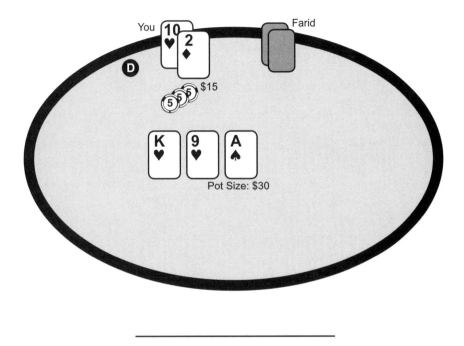

The flop comes with high cards, K♥ 9♥ A♠, and you have to think about what to do. It's fairly likely that your opponent does not have an ace in his hand and probably not even a king, because he probably would have raised if he did. There is a good chance that he does not have a draw either, because any straight draw would require two cards above a 9 and if he had such a hand, he probably would have raised before the flop. There's always the possibility that he has a flush draw, although the chances of that are low. So, unless he has a 9 in his hand, the likelihood of him having either a pair or a draw is low.

Now that you have an idea of what kind of hand your opponent is likely to have, you have to decide how to win the pot. If you check it down, unless your opponent is an extremely passive player, you will probably end up losing the pot because you will not be interested in calling any bets. Your best play is to bet right out.

SECTION

OVERVIEW

To be a winning player, you must get maximum value on your hands. You can accomplish this many different ways, depending upon the circumstances. Often doing so requires a bit of courage, because you may have to bet into some pretty scary boards. Sometimes you want to bet into a raiser hoping he will raise you, after which you can make it three bets. Other times the best way to get the most value is not to bet, but instead to entice your opponent to bet a hand weaker than what he would call with. Other times your hand is so big that all of your opponents will fold if you bet. In those situations you must be willing to check the flop, and occasionally also the turn or the river, to make the maximum on the hand. Using the check-raise can also be an effective weapon for maximizing your return.

Some of the examples in this section illustrate playing a big pair slowly before the flop, particularly in the blinds. Most of the time when you do that you will be able to make up any missed bets on the flop or the turn. When you slowplay before the flop, your hand is then disguised and you have the advantage of seeing how the hand progresses before deciding how to play your high pair. This differs from how you play a high pair in other positions, because in other positions you almost always raise to narrow the field or get more money into the pot, as it is less likely that you will be able to check-raise or somehow make it three bets on the flop or the turn.

You must also learn how and when to take control of a hand. Many times, if you are aggressive, you can force your opponents to fold better hands than yours. In the long run, there will be many situations in which neither you nor your opponents have anything. If you can win more than your fair share of those pots, it will add a lot to your bottom line. In limit hold'em, aggressive players fare a lot better than do passive players.

$10-$20 HOLD'EM: TEN-HANDED

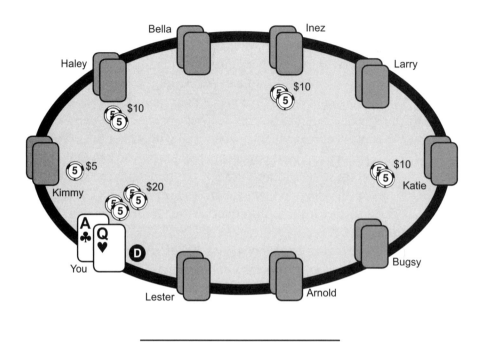

• Betting a big hand on the flop and slowplaying on the turn

You have A♣ Q♥ offsuit on the button. The players in positions No. 4 and 6 call. The next three players fold. You'd like to try to knock out the blinds and get a little dead money in the pot if possible, so you raise. A hand like A-Q offsuit plays better against fewer opponents, plus there's a good chance that you have the best hand so far.

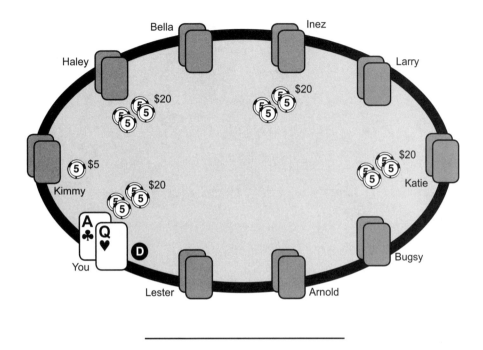

Although the small blind folds, the big blind calls your raise, as do the other two players.

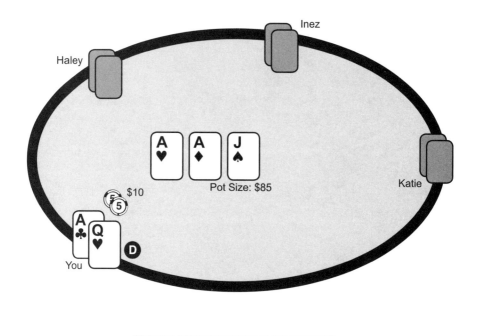

The flop, A♥ A♦ J♠, is a great one for you, but you may have trouble getting action. All the players check to you. Likely nobody has A-K or a pair of jacks because if someone did, he probably would have made it three bets to go. There's a small possibility that one of the other two players has A-J, but it's pretty unlikely, because that would require the only remaining ace and one of three remaining jacks. Many players would check with your hand in this spot, but I think that generally is a mistake. It just looks too suspicious. There's always the chance that somebody else has a worse ace than you do and that you will get a lot of action by betting. Also, any jack will probably call your bet, as well as hands like K-Q, K-J, and Q-10. Plus, many players check-raise with these draws in an attempt to win the pot without showing it down.

You bet, hoping to get check-raised. If you do get check-raised, you will just call, planning to raise on the turn. Two of the three players call your bet on the flop and the other one folds.

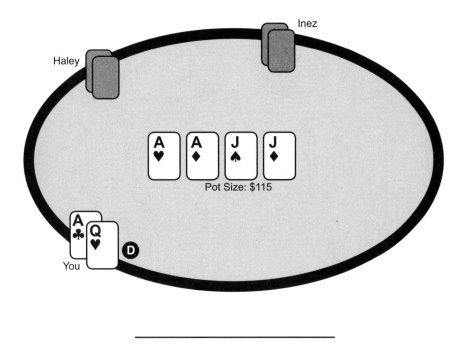

The turn pairs the jack. At this point the only hand that can beat you is pocket jacks. Both players checked to you. Your problem is that if you bet again here it's unlikely that any hand other than another ace, a jack, or pocket jacks would call.

If you check, one of the other two players may try a bluff at the pot on the river. Even if they both check, there is a good chance that one of them will call on the end if he has a king or even a queen.

You check behind them.

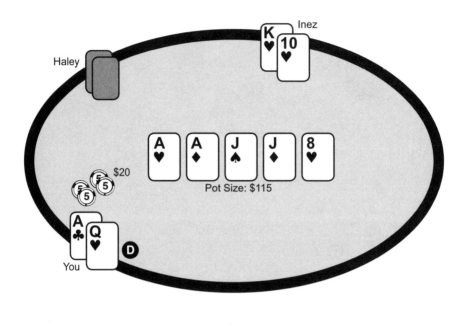

The river brings the 8♥, a blank, and both players check. You bet, hoping to get at least one call. You'd prefer not to get check-raised, because that probably would mean either that you are going to split the pot or that you are beaten.

Although the small blind folds, the remaining player does call your bet with just a king. By checking on the turn, you probably got one more bet than you would have by betting.

$10-$20 HOLD'EM: TEN-HANDED

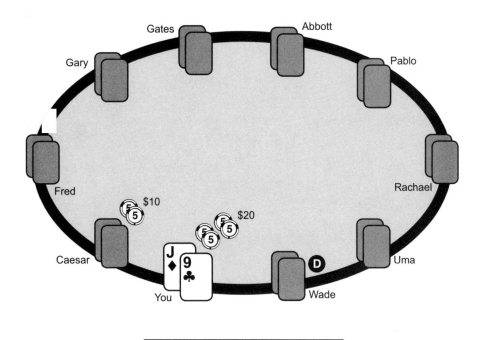

KEY CONCEPTS

• Taking control of a hand
• Small blind play
• Aggression

Everybody folds to you in the small blind. You have a mediocre hand, J♦ 9♣, but decide to raise and see if you can take the pot.
Your opponent calls.

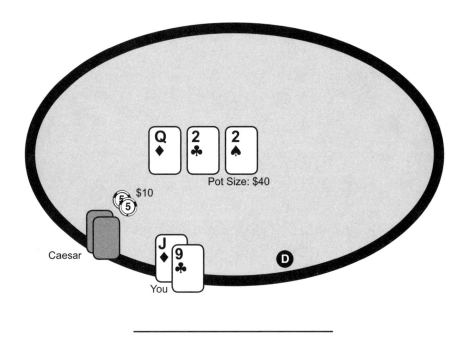

The flop comes Q♦ 2♣ 2♠, cards that that are unlikely to have helped your opponent, so you decide to do something a bit tricky that will imply your hand is even stronger than he initially suspected. You check and, as you expected, your opponent bets.

Now you make the play. You know your opponent will often bet with a mediocre hand, thinking you made a play for the pot preflop and will now give it up easily because he called and you missed the flop. You also know that the flop probably didn't help him; he probably is not paired and has no draw, so you check-raise.

If he raises you after your check-raise, you can be done with it and fold. If he calls you and you miss on the turn, you are also done with it and will check-fold. If you catch a jack or 9, you probably will bet to the end, but if you get raised on the turn or river, you probably should fold.

You figured right and your opponent folds.

$10-$20 HOLD'EM: EIGHT-HANDED

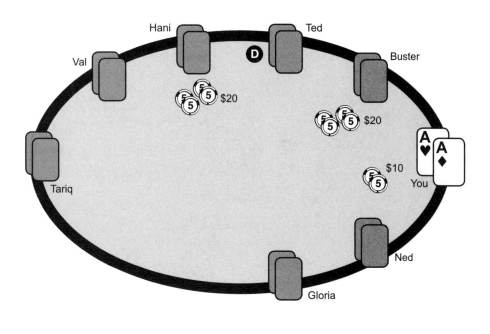

KEY CONCEPTS

- Betting for value
- Slowplaying a big pair preflop from the big blind
- Betting into the raiser to make extra bets

You have a pair of aces in the big blind. Everybody folds to the cutoff, who raises, and the small blind calls the raise. There are two ways to play this hand. You can either reraise and take the lead on the flop, or just call and play your hand according to what comes on the flop. One advantage of just calling is that the strength of your hand is concealed and you will almost always be able to raise or check-raise on the flop. Also, depending on the texture of the flop, you will often be able to get three bets by betting out and getting raised.

You flat-call.

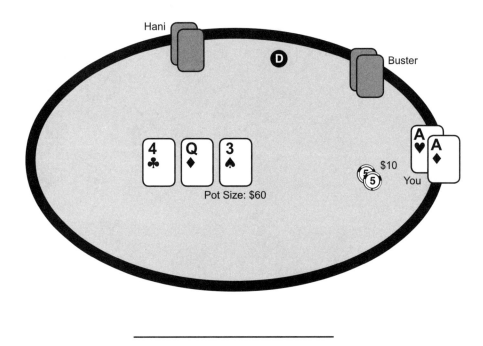

The flop comes 4-Q-3 rainbow and the small blind checks. You decide to bet, for two reasons. The first is that you hope to get raised, after which you will reraise. The second is that you feel there's a decent chance that this flop has missed the cutoff completely and she might take a free card against two callers.

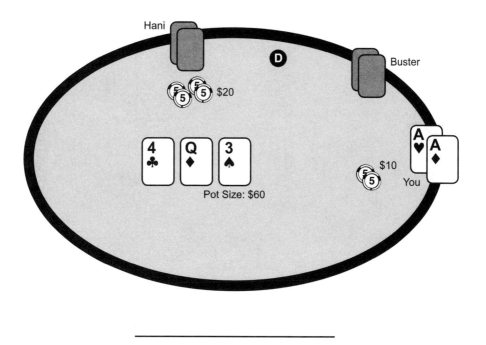

Hani raises.

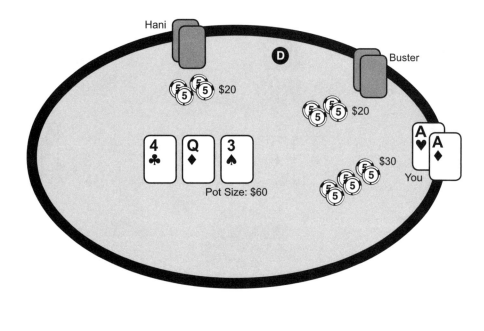

Buster calls the raise and you now get a chance to build a big pot with a very strong hand,

You reraise. This is one advantage of flat-calling with aces before the flop. Had you reraised before the flop and bet out on the flop, you probably would not get raised and you would get four small bets total instead of five on the two rounds combined.

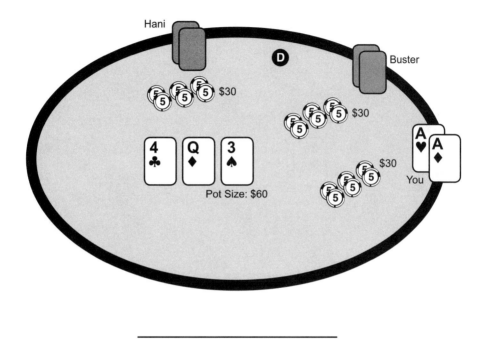

Both players call your reraise.

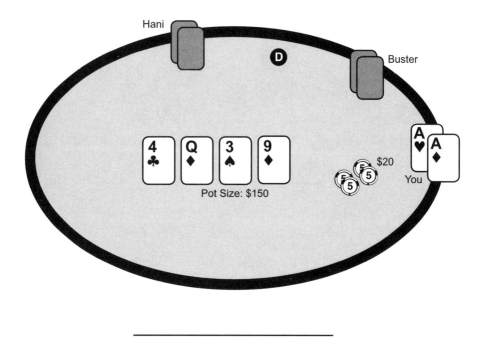

The 9♦ comes on the turn, a card that probably doesn't help either player much, although there is the possibility that it has given someone a draw. Regardless of what came, you were intending to bet.

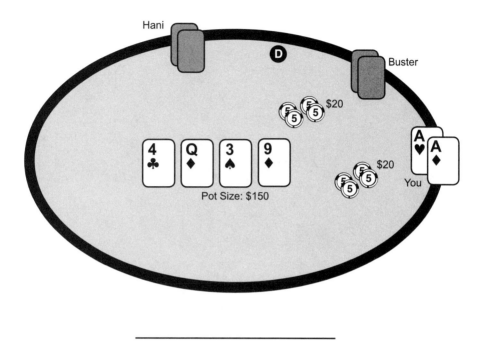

Hani folds, but the small blind calls your bet.

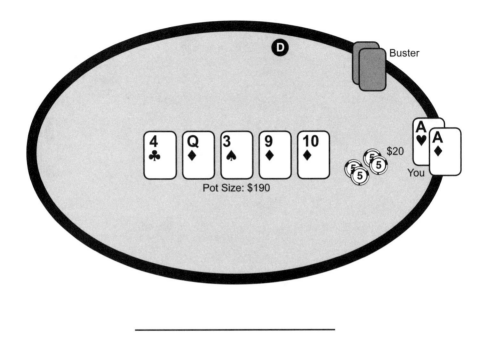

The 10♦, a scare card, comes on the river and Buster checks. You bet for value and would probably call if raised.

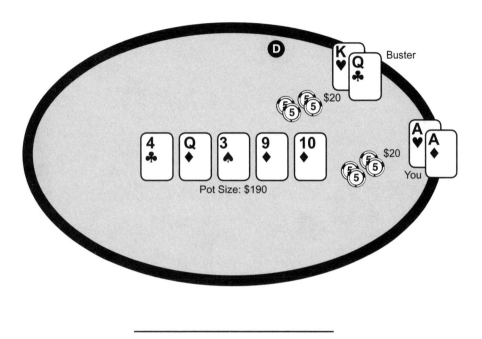

Buster calls your bet and you win a nice pot. Notice that he played this hand very conservatively.

$15-$30 HOLD'EM: NINE-HANDED

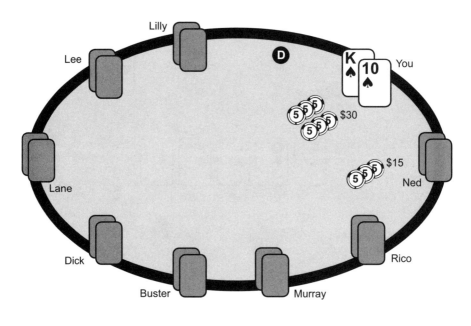

![KEY CONCEPTS]

KEY CONCEPTS

• Slowplaying a big hand
• small blind play
• being aggressive
• check-raising

You have K♠ 10♠ in the small blind and everybody folds to you. You'd like to win this hand without a contest and just take down the blinds but if you get a call, your hand is strong enough that you don't mind. You raise.

The big blind calls.

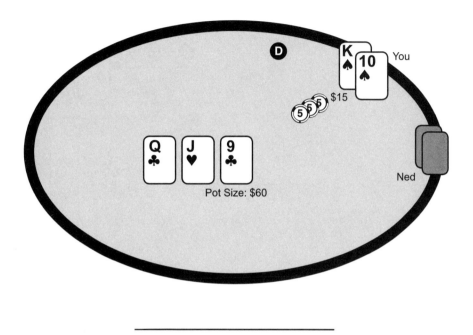

The flop comes Q♣ J♥ 9♣. You've flopped a straight. Great results. Now the problem is how to get the most out of it.

If you check, it looks suspicious. Let's say you check and your opponent bets and you call. Now what happens on the turn? If you bet then, it's likely Ned will fold. If you check now and he bets, and you check-raise, that may be the most you will get out of the pot. If you bet, he will most likely call with any card that offers a straight draw and any pair. You also might be lucky enough to get raised.

You bet and Ned calls.

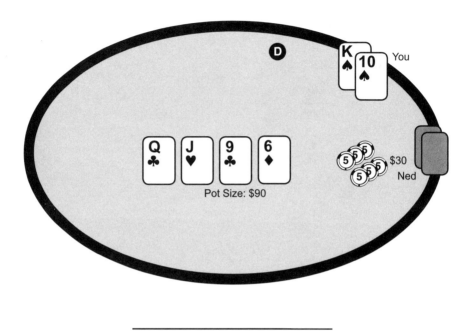

The 6♦, a blank, falls on the turn. Now is a good time to go for a check-raise. If Ned has a mediocre hand that he would have folded to a bet, he may bet hoping to knock you out. He may also check, but if he does, then you weren't that likely to have won any more by betting. He bets.

So now you check-raise and Ned folds. You probably won one more bet than you would have by betting out.

SECTION

OVERVIEW

This section contains more about blind hands. It discusses playing suited connectors and even trash hands, depending upon the implied odds. As in most sections, some examples deal with getting maximum value as well as with the importance of not giving free cards. This section also discusses attempting to isolate a likely weaker hand.

Gaining extra bets is not the only way to make money in hold'em. Many times you have to make difficult folds to save bets. A few examples illustrate tough folds. You should be able to lay down some good-looking hands before the flop as well as later in the hand. Occasionally you have to be willing to lay down top pair even if you have a great kicker.

You'll need to be aggressive when you have position; some of the examples show this. When you play aggressively, you'll encounter some check-raises from early position, because many of your opponents will assume you will be betting the flop. You need to be able to determine what kind of hand a check-raise likely represents. This section also talks about playing strong hands in tough situations against many players.

$10-$20 HOLD'EM: TEN-HANDED

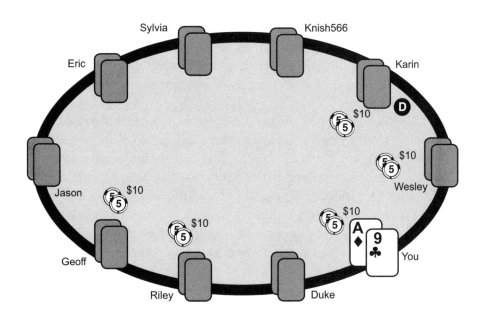

KEY CONCEPTS

• Folding top pair in the big blind

You'll often find yourself in the situation in which you have a mediocre ace in the big blind and there are a number of other players in the pot. In this particular situation, everybody has limped in and there is no reason for you to do anything but check your A♦ 9♣.

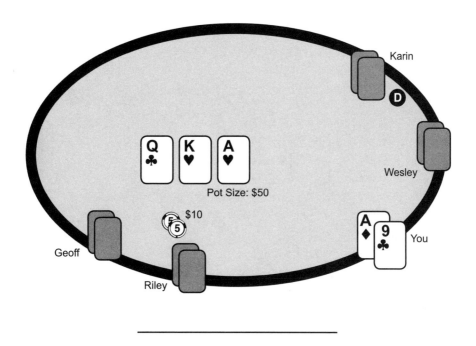

The flop comes Q-K-A, giving you a pair of aces. The small blind checks. It's unlikely that you have the best hand at this point, so you check to see what develops. An early-position caller bets.

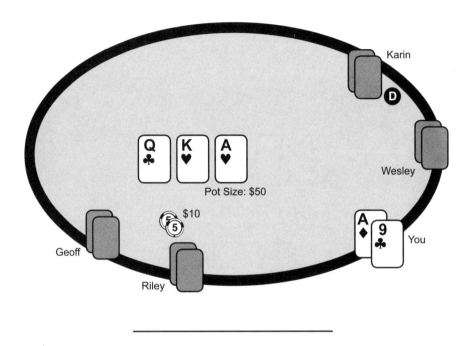

The other players fold and it comes back around to you. Now you have to try to determine the value of your hand. Let's think about the possible hands that the bettor could have that would make yours the best hand. He could have a worse ace than yours, but that is fairly unlikely since he called in very early position and there were no other callers before him. If he were to have a worse ace than yours, chances are it would be ace-small suited, but it's unlikely he would be playing that hand from early position with no other callers yet in the pot. Other possible hands that you might be able to beat would be pocket pairs below queens, but were he to have such a hand, it's extremely unlikely that he would bet it. It's also possible that he might have a hand like K-J, Q-J, Q-10, or K-10, but again, if he did, it's unlikely he would be betting it.

It's also quite likely that he could have a hand like K-Q or A-10.

He could also have A-K, A-Q, or J-10.

Because there is an excellent chance that you are in very bad shape and only a small chance that you have the best hand, it's a pretty easy fold. Many players make the mistake of calling all the way down with this hand.

$10-$20 HOLD'EM: TEN-HANDED

KEY CONCEPTS

- Folding top pair in late positin
- Aggressive late-position play
- Defensive play

You're on the button with A♦ 7♥ and everybody folds to the cutoff, who calls. Since you generally have pretty good control over the cutoff player, you raise to see if you can get heads-up. You would like to knock out both of the blinds, thereby putting some dead money in the pot, and take control of the hand.

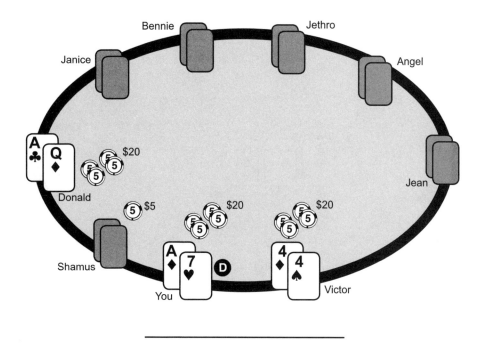

You're partially successful in that the small blind folds, but the big blind calls the raise, as does the cutoff.

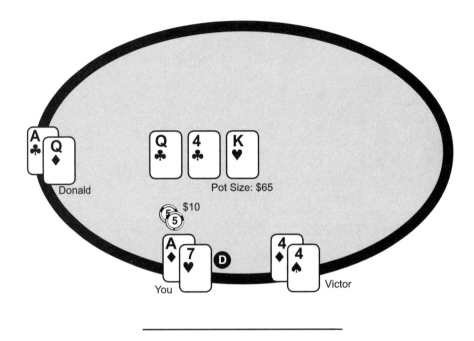

The flop comes Q♣ 4♣ K♥, and both players check to you. As is normally the case when you're aggressive before the flop and you have position, you bet the flop. In this situation, you're not betting on the strength of your hand, but rather you're hoping both opponents fold.

Unfortunately, both players call your bet.

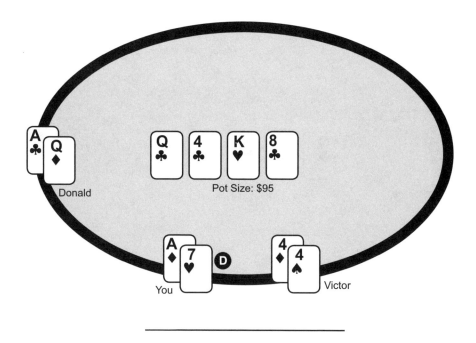

The turn brings a third club, the 8, and both players check to you. There is absolutely no reason for you to bet at this point, as you have nothing and at least one of the other players is bound to have something, since they both called your bet on the flop.

By the way, Victor has really misplayed this hand. If I had his hand, I most likely would have check-raised the flop. If I were Victor, I'd be thinking that in a raised pot against two players when I don't have any high cards, someone must have hit that flop besides me. I'd go for a check-raise, and hope that I was reraised. If for some reason I did not check-raise on the flop, I certainly would bet out on the turn when the third club fell. First of all, I wouldn't want to be giving a free card to anybody who had a club in his hand, and second, I'd be afraid that the player on the button was going to check after two people called him on the flop bet and a flush card dropped on the turn.

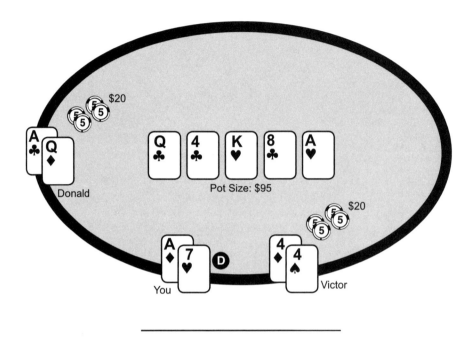

The A♥ falls on the river, Donald bets out, and Victor calls. Even if Victor had folded, you would have a difficult call on your hands. Considering that you now have to beat two players and all you have is a weak ace, it's a pretty easy fold for you.

$10-$20 HOLD'EM: TEN-HANDED

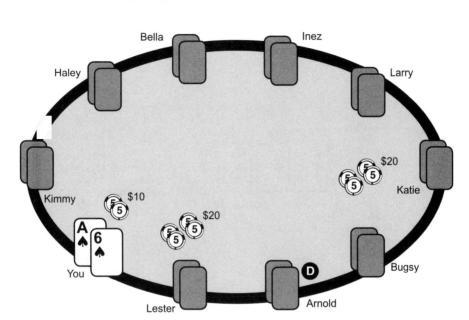

KEY CONCEPTS

• Folding top pair in the big blind

Here's a situation that should be fairly obvious to you, but I'd like to go over it to be sure you're clear. You have A♠ 6♠ in the big blind. Everybody folds to the eighth-position player, who raises. The cutoff and the button fold, and the small blind calls. It's now up to you. Although you don't like your ace, you're suited, so you call.

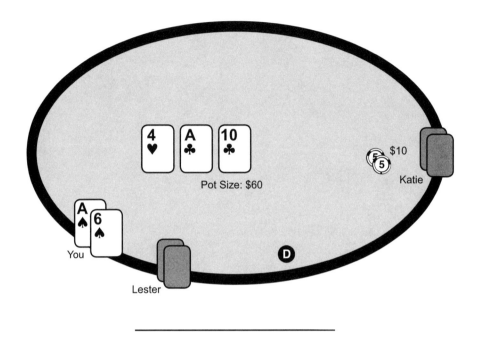

The flop comes 4♥ A♣ 10♣, and the small blind checks to you. You're not crazy about your hand, and it doesn't really matter whether you check or bet here. If you bet and get raised, you can assume that you do not have the best hand. If you check and call, you can see what happens later on this street, and if you're still around, on the turn as well.

You check, and the initial raiser bets.

The small blind calls, and although you think there is now a very good chance you do not have the best hand, you call as well. Had the small blind raised, you would have folded.

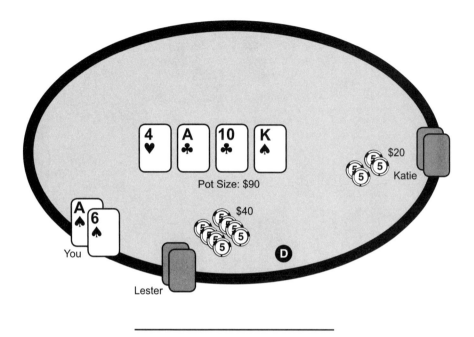

The turn brings the K♠. Lester checks, you check, and the late-position player bets. Lester check-raises.

This is an easy fold for you, as there is almost no logical combination of hands that your opponents could be holding that would allow you to have the best hand at this point.

$10-$20 HOLD'EM: TEN-HANDED

KEY CONCEPTS

- Reading a player and making a tough fold
- Slowplaying a big pair before the flop
- Isolating a probable worse hand
- Betting for value
- Not giving a free card

You have a pair of aces in the big blind, there's a caller in position No. 4, and another limper in the cutoff. The button and the small blind fold and it's up to you. Since you can almost always make a check-raise later in this spot and you want to keep the strength of your hand a secret for the time being, you check.

Another advantage of playing aces this way in this spot is that you often can bet out on the flop, get raised, and then make it three bets.

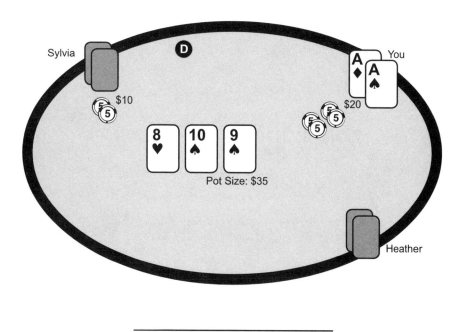

The flop comes 8♥ 10♠ 9♠, which is a bad flop for you, so you check to see what happens. Heather checks and Sylvia bets. In an unraised pot with two limpers this is a very dangerous flop for your hand. You'd like to get it heads-up if possible. You check-raise, hoping to knock out the early-position caller.

Unfortunately for you, both players call your check-raise. Since it was not three-bet, you think there is a very good chance that you have the best hand.

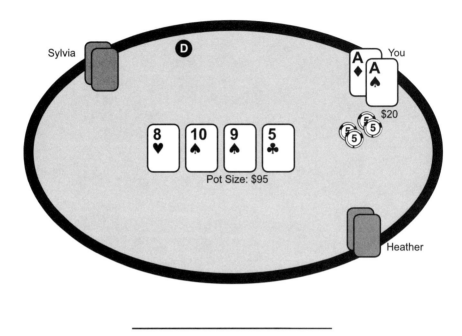

The turn brings the 5♣, a good card for you because it is unlikely to have helped either of the other players. You bet again, hoping you don't get raised. If you do get raised, you will be in a very difficult position. It's possible one of the players has flopped a set in this situation. It's also fairly likely that one of them could have flopped two pair. A hand like 6-7 or Q-J is reasonably likely as well. The likely hands that you hope they have are 7-8, J-10, Q-10, K-10, or a spade draw.

Both players call your bet. You're very relieved not to get raised and feel quite confident that you have the best hand at this point.

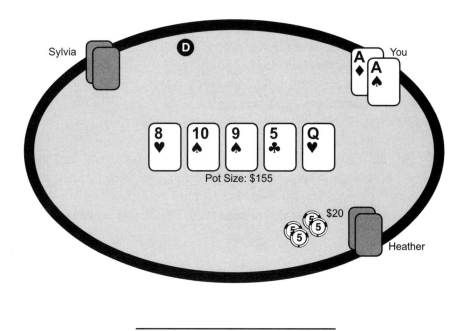

The river brings the Q♥. This is a bad card for you. If you bet, it is very unlikely you will be called by any hands that you can beat. You check, waiting to see what happens.

Unfortunately, Heather bets out. Sylvia folds and it is up to you. Now you have to think of what hands you can beat that this player would be likely to have. You know the player is fairly solid. Once the queen falls, you can no longer beat any hand with a jack in it. You can't beat any flopped straight. You can't beat any two pair.

Let's think about some of the possible hands you can beat. You can beat A-10 and K-10. The problem is that this player would not have checked either of those two hands on the flop. You can beat 7-8, but you don't think this player would call in early position with that hand and, in the unlikely event that she did, you don't think she would call your check-raise with bottom pair, bottom straight draw against two opponents in an unraised pot (which has lower pot odds). The most likely hand for Heather to have that you can beat is a busted flush draw. The problem is that you think there is very little chance that she would bet a busted flush draw into this board with the cutoff left to act and the distinct possibility that even if the cutoff folds, you are probably going to call.

You're getting a bit less than 8 to 1 odds to call this bet. All things considered, you think there is less than 1 chance in 8 that you have the best hand.

You fold.

By the way, had the middle-position player checked and the player in the cutoff bet, you probably should call, because it would be much more likely for someone to bluff into this board if two players had already checked to her and she had no other way to win the pot.

$10-$20 HOLD'EM: TEN-HANDED

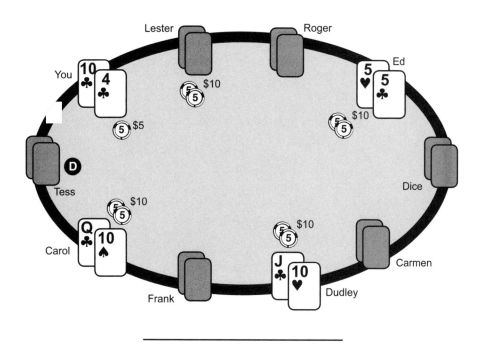

KEY CONCEPTS

- Folding top pair
- Implied odds
- Playing a trash hand

Here's an example of calling a small bet with a bad hand due to high implied odds and flopping something other than what you called for. Many people get trapped when they do this, so it is something to be very careful about. You have 10-4 suited in the small blind in an unraised multiway pot. You should call here with any two cards for a number of reasons. First, you're getting great implied odds. Second, if you hit your hand it will be disguised and you should be able to get extra bets in. Third, if you miss the hand it should be easy to get away from. Fourth, if you hit the hand and then have to show it down, it will be good for your image.

You call and the big blind checks, making this a five-way pot.

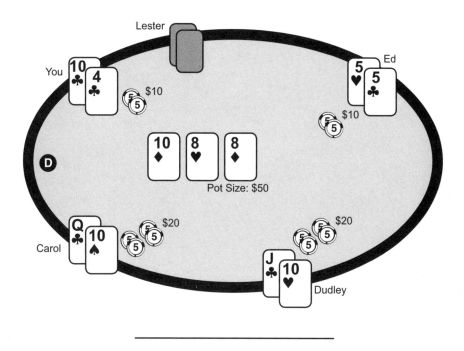

The flop comes 10-8-8. In this situation, it's not unlikely that you could have an 8. You bet your tens knowing some players might give you credit for a better hand than you actually have. The big blind folds, Ed calls, Dudley raises, and Carol calls the raise.

Now you have to think about whether to call the raise. How are you going to win this pot? Your hand is almost certainly no good. That means you will probably have to catch a 10 to have a chance, and even then you will probably be splitting the pot with a 10 with a better kicker. For you to have the best hand here, your opponents almost all have to be drawing. Any 10 probably has you drawing to split. Any 8 has you in bad shape. A draw with two overcards is the best you can hope to be up against, but with three other players in the pot, it is not likely that all three have that. Even in the unlikely chance that you have the best hand now, your opponents probably have so many outs that you are a big underdog to win the hand. Your best move is to fold.

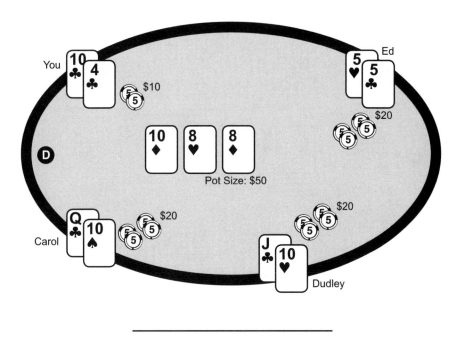

You fold and Ed calls. Let's follow the action and see what your opponents do and how the rest of the hand plays out.

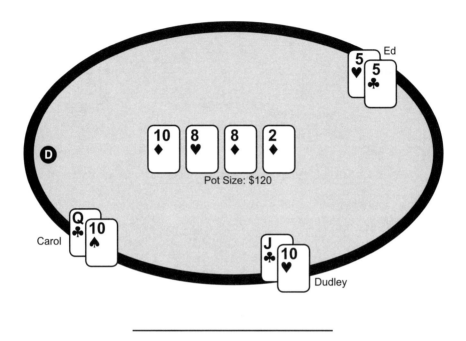

Pot Size: $120

The turn brings the 2♦. Ed checks. Dudley checks. Carol checks, but she should bet here because she doesn't want to give the other players a free draw at a diamond or an overcard. If she gets raised, she can safely fold and not worry too much about losing her free draw to a 10 because she was enough of an underdog that she had more to lose by giving a free card than she cost himself by taking her own free card away.

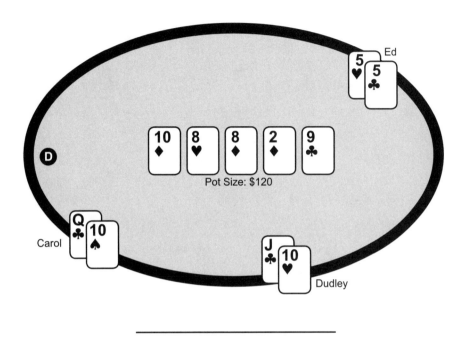

The river brings the 9♣. Ed checks. Dudley could bet here but he is likely to get called only by a better hand than his. Carol also checks but, again, should bet for value. Since both other players have checked to her twice, it is unlikely that either of them has a hand as strong as K-10, the minimum required to beat her hand.

$10-$20 HOLD'EM: TEN-HANDED

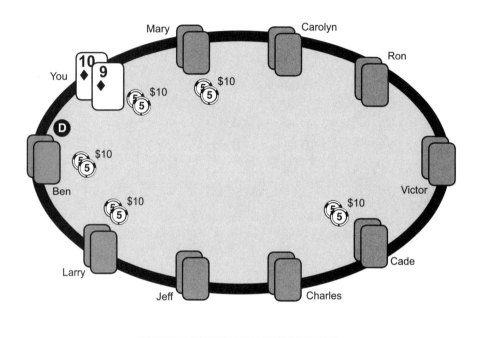

  KEY CONCEPTS

- Folding top pair
- Playing a suited connector from the small blind
- Considering a check-raise from the small blind in a multiway pot

Here's an example of folding top pair with a mediocre kicker. With three players having limped, you call with 10♦ 9♦ in the small blind because your hand is a good multiway hand and you're getting more than the necessary odds. You're trying to hit a draw, a made hand, a set, or two pair. You're not really looking to hit one pair in this situation. The big blind checks behind you.

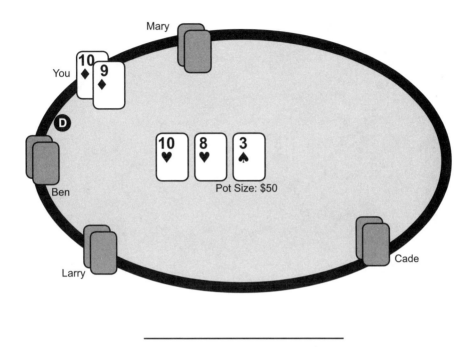

The flop comes 10♥ 8♥ 3♠. Although you flop top pair, you decide to check and see what develops. With this many players, you will almost certainly get a chance to check-raise. You intend to check-raise if all players check and only Larry or Ben bets. You will check-raise under those circumstances for two reasons. The first is that you want to narrow the field. The second is that you may well have the best hand.

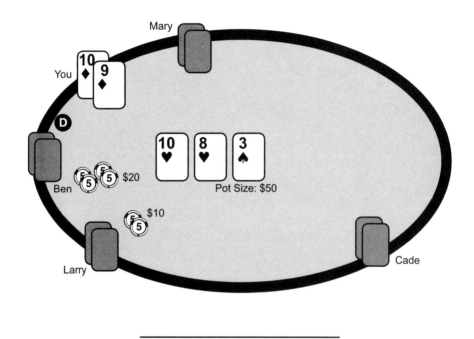

The next two players check, Larry bets, and Ben, the player on the button raises. Now you have to think about what you can beat. Any 10 with a kicker higher than a 9 has you in terrible shape. A 10-8 has you drawing to three 9s or a running pair above the 10s. How likely is a pair of 10s with a lower kicker than yours? That would be a 10-7 or lower. Not many players play that kind of hand unless they are in the blind. Not only that, but you are facing a raise. The best you can reasonably hope for is one player with A-8 and the other with a draw. It is much more likely that at least one of the players has a better 10 than yours like J-10, Q-10, K-10, or A-10. There are also three other players left to act after you if you call.

Even if you currently have the best hand, which is doubtful, a large portion of the deck will beat you. Also, you have the worst position and don't know where you stand. Your best play here is to fold. If you do decide to play (which I don't recommend), you should probably reraise, hoping to narrow the field to you and the player on the button and hoping that he is on a draw.

$10-$20 HOLD'EM: TEN-HANDED

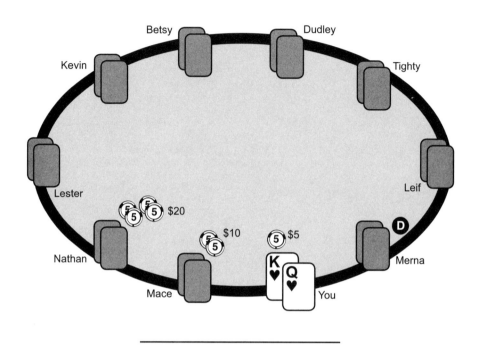

KEY CONCEPTS

• Folding a good hand preflop to a raise from early position

You have K-Q suited in the small blind and the under-the-gun player raises. Everyone else folds to you. You have a great hand for a number of situations, but not this particular one. Here are the problems with calling this raise. First, you're in the worst possible position for the entire hand. Second, you have a hand that plays well against a large field and at best it will be a three-way pot. Third, the raiser is under the gun, which makes it fairly likely he's holding a hand that has you completely dominated, like pocket aces, pocket kings, A-K, or A-Q.

Many players fall into the trap of seeing all the potential of this kind of hand and not accurately assessing the entire situation. You always have to consider what likely hands you will be playing against before you decide what to do. Even if you were on the button, this would be a borderline call against decent players.

You have an easy fold in this situation. If four or so players had called before it got to you, you probably *would* call the raise. Also, in a short-handed game you'd certainly call the raise. But not here.

$10-$20 HOLD'EM: NINE-HANDED

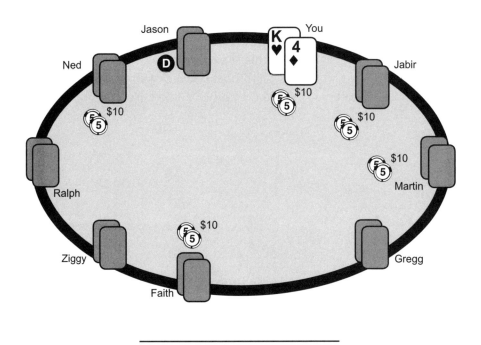

KEY CONCEPTS

- Folding top pair in a multiway pot
- Calling preflop with trash

You have K-4 offsuit in the small blind and three people call, so you are getting 9 to 1 odds on your call. You also don't want to appear too tight, so you call. The big blind checks.

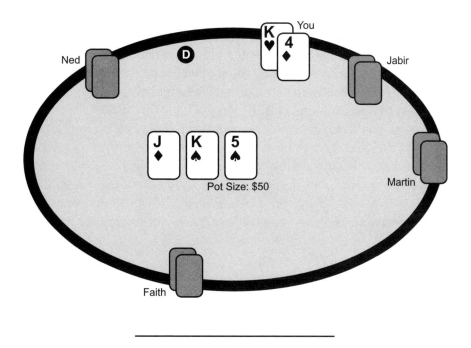

Pot Size: $50

The flop comes J♦ K♠ 5♠. What should you do? Consider what your opponents might have. It's pretty likely that one of them has a king, and if so, he has you in very bad shape. Since the pot was not raised, but there were early- and middle-position callers, it is quite possible that one of them has a hand like K-J. If nobody has a king, at least one person probably has a good draw. If you bet out, you will most likely get more than one caller and there is a good chance you will be raised. If you get raised, you will probably call one bet and then fold to any bet if you don't hit your kicker. Even if you do hit your kicker, you stand a good chance of losing to either a flush or a straight on the end. Your best move against solid players is to check and see what develops.

The first two players check behind you, the middle-late-position player bets, and the player on the button folds. Because you don't know where you're at and there are still two other players to act behind you (and taking into consideration why you decided to check initially), you fold.

If, instead, the middle-late-position player had checked and the button had bet, and you knew the player on the button would bet many hands worse than yours, you might check-raise him. You'd be trying to get it heads-up with a possible bluffer or drawer by making it two bets to everyone else. If you got called by one of the other players, you'd be very cautious on the turn. If only the button called your raise, you'd continue to lead on the turn.

It's possible that one of the players who checked is slowplaying two pair or trips, but if you got reraised by one of them it would be an easy fold. If everyone else folded and the button reraised, you'd have to use your knowledge of the player in deciding how to proceed.

$10-$20 HOLD'EM: SEVEN-HANDED

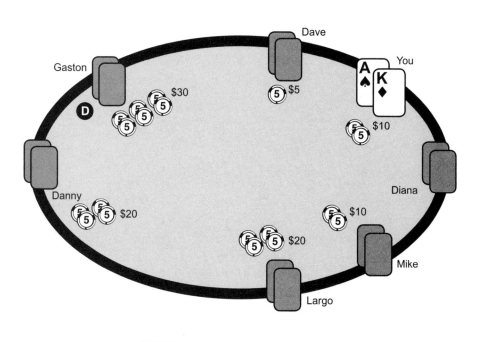

KEY CONCEPTS

• Evaluating a strong hand in a tough situation against many players

You're in the big blind with A-K offsuit. The player in position No. 4 has limped in, the player in position No. 5 has raised, the cutoff has called the raise, and the button three-bets it. The small blind folds and now it's up to you. Normally your hand would be very strong, but in a situation like this it almost turns into a trouble hand. With an early-position caller, a middle-position raiser, another caller, and then a reraiser after that, it's fairly likely that at least one of those players has a high pair. It's also quite likely that many of the cards you need to make a hand are already accounted for in other players' hands. There is no reason to make it four bets, but you're not going to fold either, so you just call.

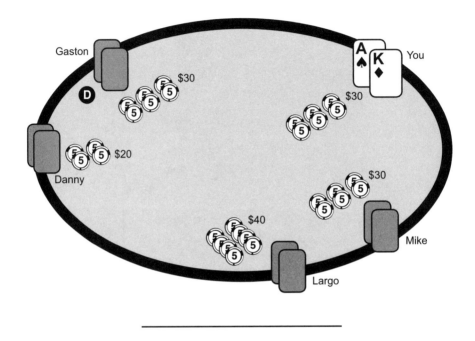

The player in position No. 4 calls as well, and the initial raiser caps it.

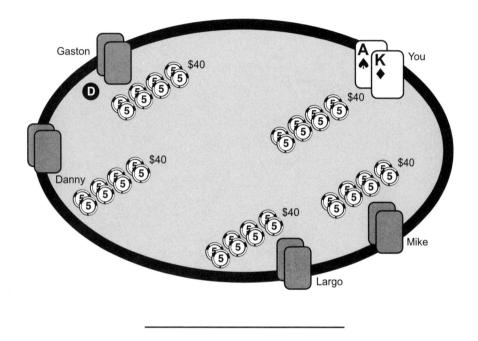

Everybody calls.

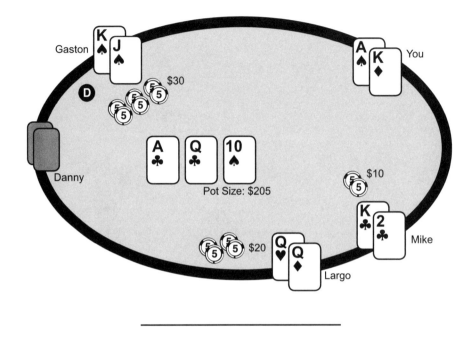

Pot Size: $205

The flop comes A♣ Q♣ 10♠ and, although you flop aces with a king kicker, you're not crazy about your hand, so you check to see what happens. Mike bets, he gets raised by Largo, Danny folds, and Gaston reraises. Now it's up to you.

Well, you certainly got a lot of information. Now you have to figure out what your hand is worth. Anybody with pocket aces, pocket queens, or pocket 10s has you in terrible shape. Anybody with A-Q, A-10, or Q-10 has you in terrible shape as well. Anybody holding K-J has a straight and has you drawing to two runners or a split. If you happen to hit your second pair, anybody with a jack in his hand makes a straight. Finally, there's a flush draw out there as well.

This is an easy fold. Muck your hand and let the others duke it out. As you can see, you were drawing almost dead.

$10-$20 HOLD'EM: TEN-HANDED

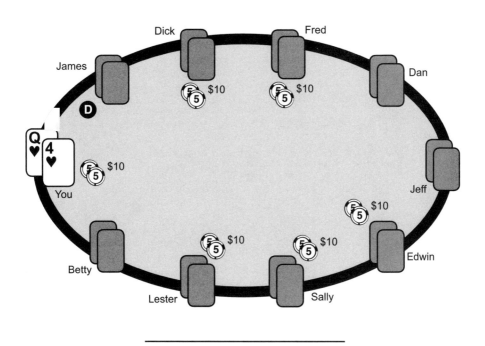

KEY CONCEPTS

• Bluffing on the river
• Playing a marginal hand
• Playing a draw aggressively
• Semibluffing

Although Q-4 suited is not a hand I generally recommend playing, there are some circumstances in which it is warranted. This is a good example. You're in late position and three players have limped in before you. You call, expecting both blinds to come in as well. It's good to play a volume pot cheaply with this kind of hand because you're trying to make a big hand with it.

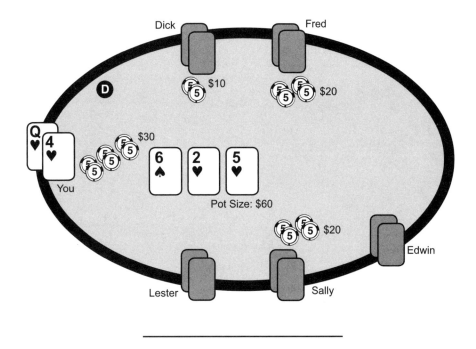

The flop is 6♠ 2♥ 5♥. This is an excellent flop for you. You've flopped a draw to both a flush and gutshot straight, giving you 12 likely outs, with the possibility of three more if a queen can win you the pot. The small blind bets out and is raised by the big blind. Edwin folds, Sally, the player in position No. 6, calls, and Lester folds. It's up to you. Since you have so many potential outs and the best position, you make it three bets. You'll be fine if someone caps it. By making it three bets, you may have a chance to take a free card on the turn if you miss. Even if you miss on the turn and someone bets in front of you, you won't mind calling as you probably still will have quite a few outs.

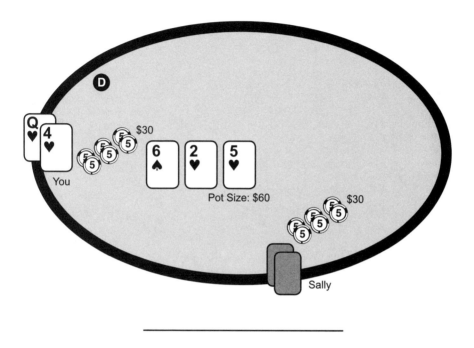

To your surprise, both blinds fold and only Sally calls your raise.

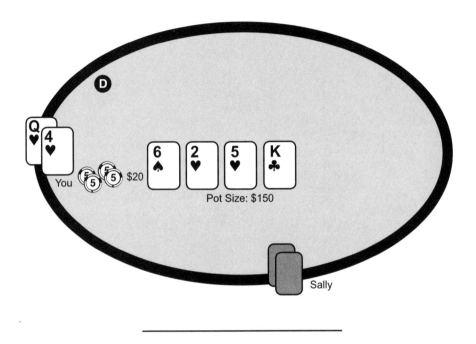

The K♣ comes on the turn. Although this card doesn't improve your hand at all, your opponent isn't showing any strength, so after she checks to you, you bet again. You are hoping to win this pot whether you improve or not. You think there is a good chance that Sally hasn't yet made a pair and is still drawing, perhaps to a better flush than you are. She decides to call.

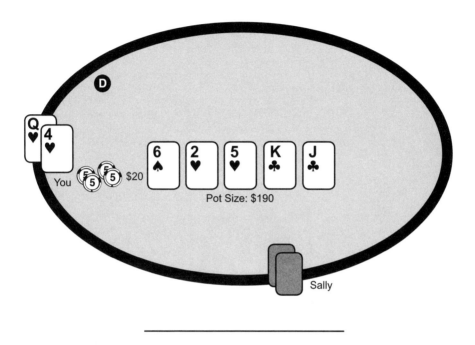

The J♣, another card that is unlikely to have helped your opponent, falls on the river. If she checked to you, you were going to bet regardless of what came, so, when she checks, that's what you do.

Sally folds and you win a very nice pot with queen high. Notice that aggressive play, a bit of semibluffing, and a river bluff helped you to win this large pot. Had you played more conservatively, you would have lost it.

SECTION

OVERVIEW

This section includes quite a few different concepts. There is more discussion on playing out of the blinds. It examines further how to get the most value out of hands. This includes betting some marginal hands for value and betting out with the hope of being raised. It also talks about the vital concept of free cards. If you give a free card to a player who would not have called you if you bet and you end up losing the pot because of it, unless you would make more in the long run by letting him see the card for free, you have made a big mistake. One way you could make more in the long run is when your opponent has very few outs but has many cards that would make him a second-best hand with which he will put more bets into the pot.

Another concept this section covers is continuation bets. That's the practice of following up a preflop raise with a bet on the flop. Although you don't have to bet the flop every time you raise preflop, you should get in the habit of doing so often, even if you have very little. You will win a decent percentage of the time when your opponents fold, and it's good for your image.

This section also talks about isolation and gaining control of a hand. Reraising or three-betting is a great way to gain control of a hand. It can also be very effective if you want to isolate a weaker hand in an attempt to play the pot heads-up or against only two opponents.

It also covers marginal calls, including why you might call on the flop when you are quite sure you don't have the best hand. It presents some situations in which it pays to play overcards very strongly. And, finally, it discusses playing your opponents according to their playing style, thinking ahead, and avoiding traps.

$10-$20 HOLD'EM: TEN-HANDED

KEY CONCEPTS

- Don't give free cards
- Three-betting preflop to gain control
- Continuation bets

You have A-Q offsuit in the cutoff. A player raised under the gun and everybody has folded to you. With any pair 10s or above, A-K, or A-Q, you will usually make it three bets under these circumstances. With those hands, you would like to play heads-up and get some extra dead money in the pot. Your hand plays a lot better against one opponent than against two or three. If you flat-call the raise, there is a decent chance that the player on the button will call and also that either or both of the blinds will call as well. Your best protection against this is to three-bet.

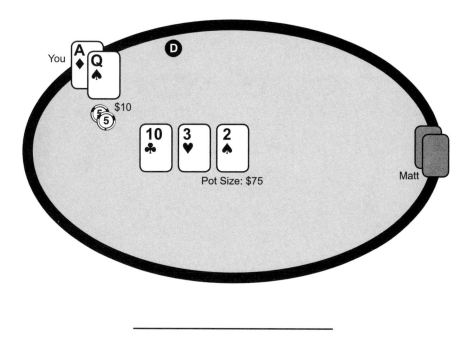

As you hoped, everybody except the under-the-gun player folds; you were successful in isolating that player and in getting some dead money into the pot. The flop comes 10♣ 3♥ 2♠ and the initial raiser checks. Now it's up to you to evaluate the situation. You know that your opponent might raise from early position with A-J, K-Q, and K-J suited. Of course, he would also raise with a high pair, A-K, or A-Q. At this stage you're not really sure what hand he has, but, so long as he has not shown strength, be aggressive and give yourself a chance to win the pot without making a hand.

Provided Matt does not have a pair, this flop is very unlikely to have helped his hand. Although he raised under the gun, he did not reraise you before the flop, and he has checked on the flop. You're going to play your hand for the best hand until you have evidence to the contrary. You also want to give Matt a chance to fold if he has either A-K or A-Q. You bet.

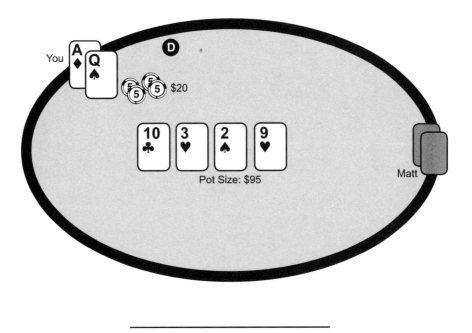

Matt calls your flop bet and the turn brings the 9♥. He checks to you. There is no reason to believe that this card has helped his hand, so you bet again, hoping to win the pot. This time it works out; your opponent folds.

$10-$20 HOLD'EM: TEN-HANDED

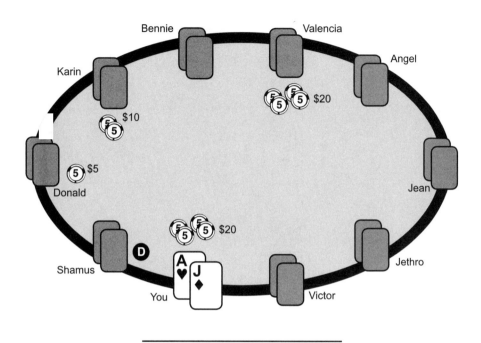

KEY CONCEPTS

• Thinking ahead
• Not trapping yourself
• Not giving free cards

You have A♥ J♦ in the cutoff. The player under the gun folds and Valencia, in position No 4., raises. The next four players fold and it's up to you. If you had A-Q or better, you frequently would reraise, but A-J can be a trap hand in this spot. If you know that the raiser commonly overplays his hands, you might reraise with A-J and play it for the best hand, but this player is fairly solid and you think there is a decent chance that she has you beaten.

You just call the raise and wait to see what happens on the flop. The button and both blinds fold.

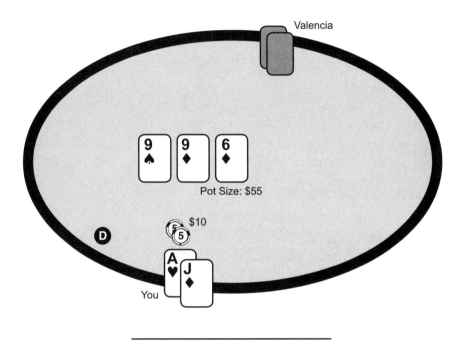

The flop, 9♠ 9♦ 6♦, probably didn't help your opponent and she checks to you. If you were the early-position raiser, you usually would bet this flop. If you checked, it usually would be because you were trying for a check-raise.

Now you have to decide whether Valencia has indeed missed her hand or whether she is trying to trap you. You still feel that there is a good possibility that you don't have the best hand, but if you check here, you think it decreases the chances that you will end up winning the pot.

Your best shot to win the hand is to bet here. There's very little risk because if you get check-raised, you'll just throw it away. If your opponent calls you and checks on the turn, you will most likely bet. If an ace comes on the turn, you probably will check, because the most likely hands for her to have if she calls your bet on the flop but does not check-raise you are A-K or A-Q. It doesn't make sense that Valencia would check-call with any pair on a flop like that, unless she has pocket aces, pocket kings, pocket 6s, or a hand like A-9 suited, and is waiting to check-raise you. If an ace falls on the turn and she checks to you, betting would not be a big mistake, but you would be prepared to fold if you got check-raised. Another reason that you might check on the turn if an ace falls is to induce a bluff from your opponent on the river.

If an ace fell on the turn and you both checked, and then your opponent checked the river, you would certainly bet on the end. If an ace fell on the turn and you both checked and your opponent then bet the river, you would just call the bet and not raise. That's because there are very few hands that she could call your raise with that would not have you beat.

The reason you bet the flop is because you'd like to give Valencia the chance to fold hands like K-Q and K-J. There's also a small possibility that she might fold a hand like A-J or even A-Q. Valencia calls and we see the turn.

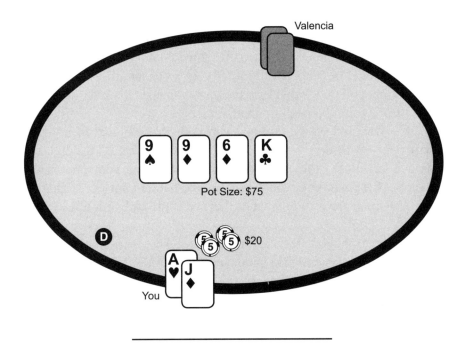

A king falls on the turn and Valencia checks to you. You bet and she folds. Your best guess is that she had either A-Q or the same hand as you did. In the former case, you won without having the best hand. In the latter, you won all of a pot you would have split by checking.

$10-$20 HOLD'EM: TEN-HANDED

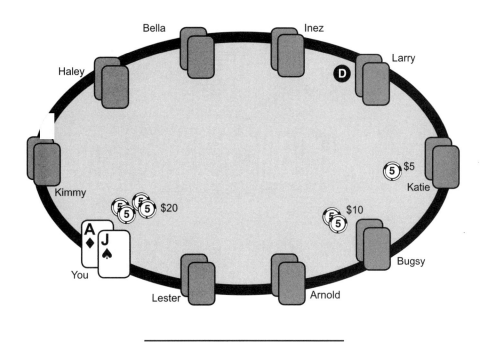

KEY CONCEPTS

- Betting marginal hands for value
- Continuation bets
- Reading your opponent
- Not giving free cards

You raise from position No. 5 with A-J offsuit. Everybody folds around to the big blind, who calls.

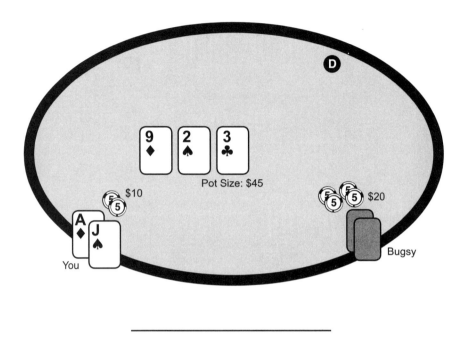

The flop comes 9-2-3 rainbow. The big blind checks, you bet, and the big blind check-raises you.

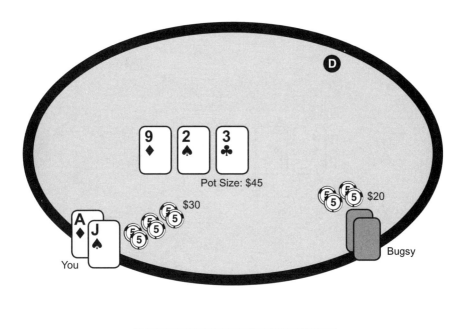

A couple of factors make you suspicious of this check-raise. The first is that you know this player is capable of trying to steal the pot, especially in a heads-up situation. The second is that the flop looks very unlikely to have helped you since the most likely hand for you to have was something like A-K, A-Q, A-J, or K-Q. If Bugsy puts you on one of those hands, he might think he can get you to lay it down. You feel there is a very good chance that you have the best hand in spite of your opponent's check-raise. Therefore you decide to play it aggressively and reraise.

Bugsy calls.

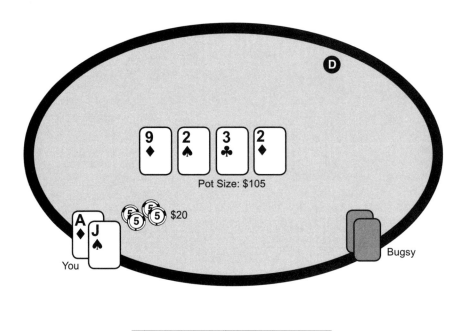

The turn pairs the deuce and Bugsy checks. You are not particularly afraid of this card and you still think there is a very good chance that you have the best hand, so to avoid giving a free card, and to get value on your hand, you bet again.

Bugsy again calls.

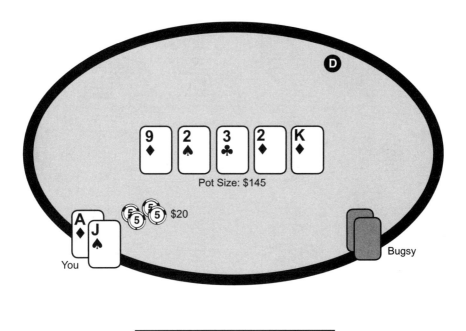

The K♦ comes on the river and Bugsy checks. You think it unlikely that the king helped him, but you also think there is a small chance that he initially paired the 3 or has a pair of 4s or some other small pair. Had the river card been a queen or below, you probably would check on the end. But the king is the kind of card that could have helped most of the hands you would have been betting that did not already beat a small pair, so you bet on the end to help win the pot just in case he has you beat. After all, it's not entirely unlikely that you would have played A-K the same way that you would play a high pair in the hole.

You're not sure if you were betting with the best hand all along or if the king scared your opponent and he folded a small pair, but, regardless, you win the pot.

$10-$20 HOLD'EM: TEN-HANDED

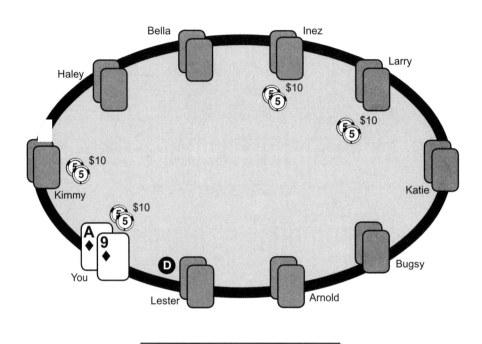

KEY CONCEPTS

- Don't give free cards
- Small blind play
- Betting out to get maximum value

Here you have a pretty good hand, A-9 suited, in the small blind. Two players have limped from middle position. Some people like to raise with a suited ace like this from either of the blinds, but I generally don't feel that is a very good play. Although it does make the pot bigger and entices people to stay in longer when you flop a flush draw, most of the time you won't help your hand on the flop and, since you are in early position, you are placing yourself in an awkward situation if you miss the flop.

You just call and the big blind checks.

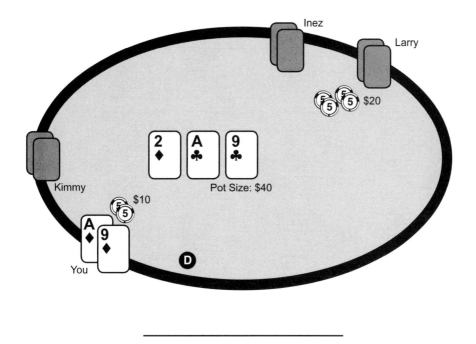

The flop comes 2♦ A♣ 9♣ and you bet out, hoping to get raised. Your reasoning is as follows. In pots in which nobody has shown any strength before the flop and some medium or low cards flop, it's not uncommon for one of the blinds to bet a weak hand into the rest of the field. You're hoping that one of your opponents picks up on this and tries to put pressure on you. You're also hoping that one of your opponents has an ace and, if so, you expect that he will raise you.

The big blind folds, the next player folds, and the last player raises.

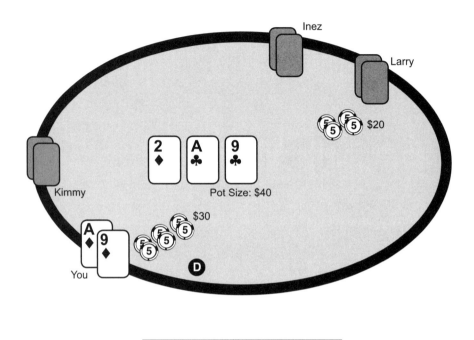

This is exactly what you hoped would happen, and you're not going to get tricky. You reraise. The reason that you reraise here is because you do not want to give a free card. There are two clubs on board so it's possible that the raiser has a flush draw and is expecting to check on the turn if another club does not come. And there also is the possibility that, since both other players have folded, Larry does not believe that you have an ace and is just trying to draw out on you with a hand like K♣ Q♦.

The main point here is that you bet out hoping to get raised so that you can reraise and get extra value on your hand. Larry calls the reraise.

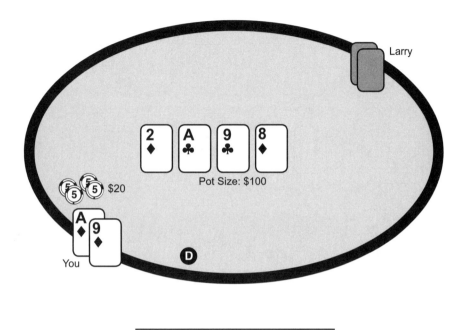

The 8♦ comes on the turn. You bet out and get called.

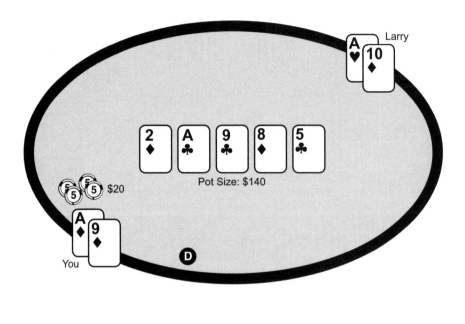

The river is another club, the 5, which completes the possible flush draw, but you bet out, trying to get value on your top two pair. Note that you bet your strong hand even though a third club fell. Many players become worried that they are beaten by a flush and check the river in a situation like this. Since limit games are all about getting maximum value, you need to bet in this spot. If you get raised, you can make a decision about whether to call, but most of the time you would.

$10-$20 HOLD'EM: TEN-HANDED

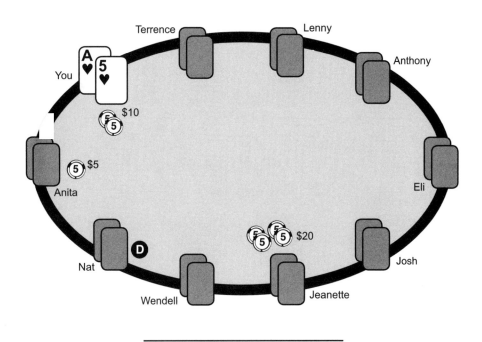

KEY CONCEPTS

• Calling on the flop with what you think is the worst hand
• Big blind play
• Not giving a free card
• Betting for value

You have a decent hand in the big blind, A♥ 5♥. Everybody folds to the player in position No. 8, who raises. The cutoff, the button, and the small blind fold as well. Now it's up to you. There is a reasonable chance that you have the better hand, but you will be acting first throughout and, even if you flop an ace, will probably not know where you stand. Although you're certainly not going to fold this hand, you'd rather not be too aggressive until you see the flop and are able to make a better assessment of the situation.

You call the raise.

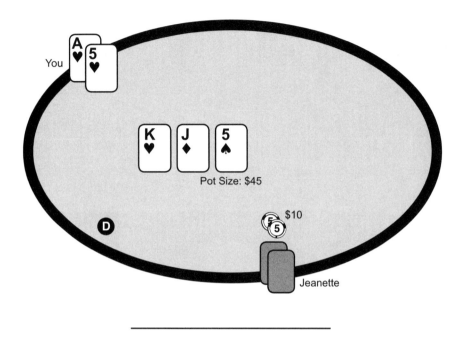

The flop is K♥ J♦ 5♠, giving you a pair of 5s with an ace kicker and a backdoor flush draw. You check to the raiser. She bets and it's up to you to call. There's a chance that you have the best hand here and if you call you may get a free card on the turn.

You call.

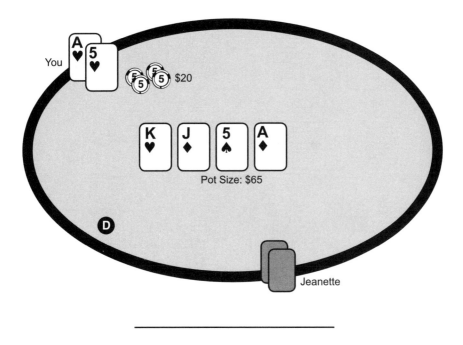

The turn brings an ace, giving you two pair. You're pretty sure that you have the best hand now and you're not interested in giving a free card. If Jeanette has a hand like 10-9, J-10, K-10, Q-J, or any two diamonds, she might check behind you if you check. Because you think you have the best hand, and you think she probably has enough to call if you bet, and because you don't want to give a free card, you bet out.

Your opponent calls.

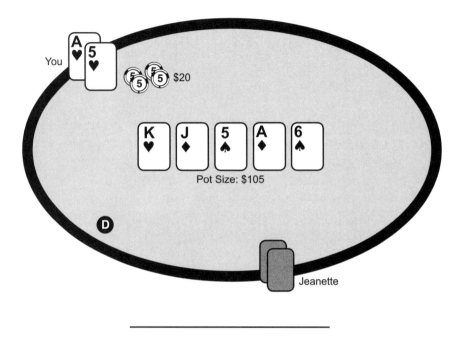

The river brings a blank and you bet out again, hoping that Jeanette has enough to call you.

She doesn't, and folds.

$10-$20 HOLD'EM: TEN-HANDED

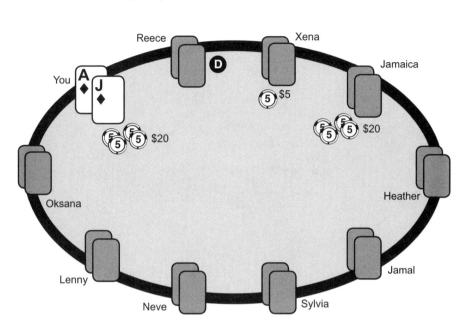

![KEY CONCEPTS]

KEY CONCEPTS

• Don't give a free card because of a scare card

This fairly straightforward example illustrates the importance of betting your hand all the way through for value unless you have some compelling reason not to. You raise in late position with A♦ J♦ after everybody folds to you. The button and the small blind fold and the big blind calls your raise.

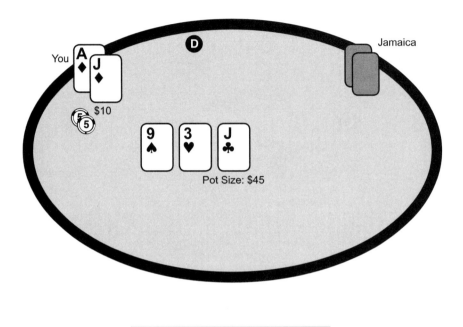

The flop is 9♠ 3♥ J♣, giving you top pair. The big blind checks to you. Although some players make what they think is a tricky check here, that is not a good idea. Any king or queen can put you in bad shape. Also, Jamaica may have an open-ended or gutshot straight draw. You don't want to give those hands a free card and you do want to get any bets you can out of him on the flop. You also like to bet your strong hands in this situation so that your opponents will be more likely to fold when you don't have anything and you bet.

You bet, and your opponent calls.

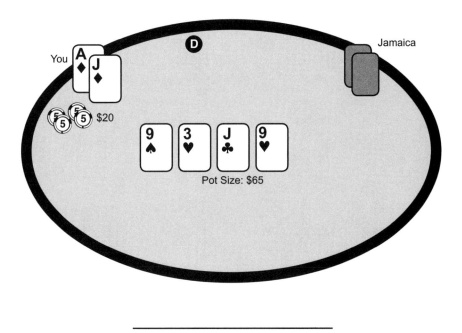

The 9♥ on the turn pairs the board and Jamaica checks to you. The reason for this example is because some players worry that the 9 has given their opponent trips and decide to check in this spot. That is a very bad play, because there are far too many hands that would call your bet that you are otherwise giving a free card to. Also, most of those hands will not call you and will not bluff at you on the river.

Don't fall into the trap of being afraid of any scare card that falls and therefore miss betting your hands for value.

You bet and your opponent folds. Many times, though, you would get a call from hands like Q-10, K-10, 10-8, any jack, any 3, or two hearts.

$10-$20 HOLD'EM: EIGHT-HANDED

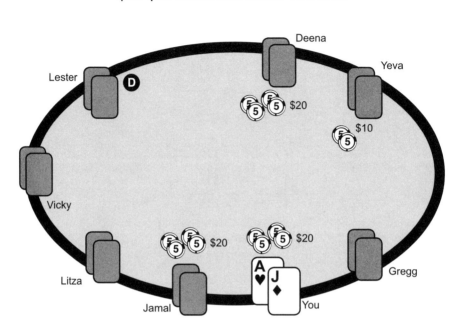

KEY CONCEPTS

- Continuation bets
- Not giving free cards
- Betting marginal hands for value

You have A-J offsuit in position No. 4 and the player under the gun has folded. You raise, and the player to your left calls. The other players fold until it gets to the small blind, who calls. The big blind folds.

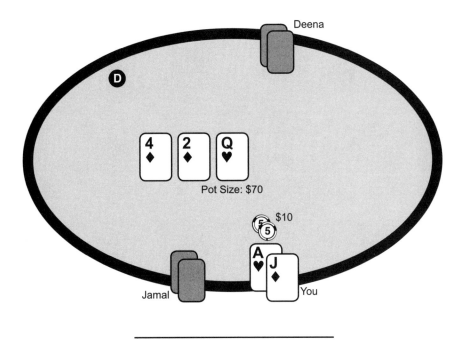

The flop comes 4♦ 2♦ Q♥ and the small blind checks. Although the flop completely missed you, since you raised before the flop, you continue betting.

171

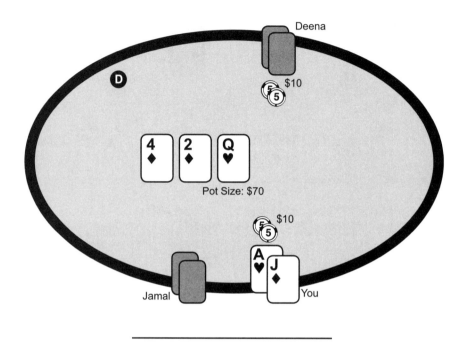

The player on your left folds, and the small blind calls.

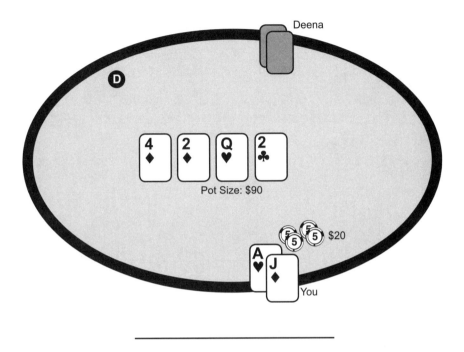

The turn pairs the board and the small blind again checks to you. You still have nothing, but Deena has not indicated any strength. Chances are you have the best hand. Checking here doesn't make any sense at all. If you bet and get check-raised it's an easy fold. If you check here and Deena bets the river you're going to call, so you'd be much better off betting here and checking the river if your opponent calls.

You bet, and Deena folds.

$10-$20 HOLD'EM: NINE-HANDED

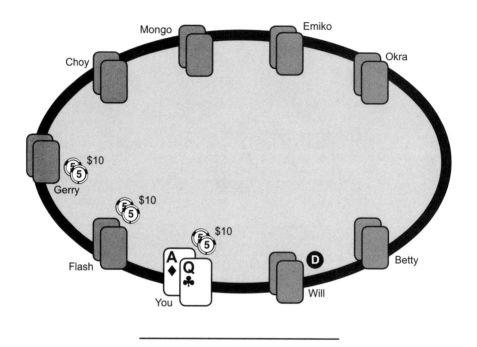

- Playing the players
- Not giving free cards

You are in the small blind with one caller from under the gun, and everybody else has folded to you. There is a decent chance that you have the best hand with A-Q offsuit, but because you are in the worst position and can probably get a check-raise on the flop if you want it, you just call.

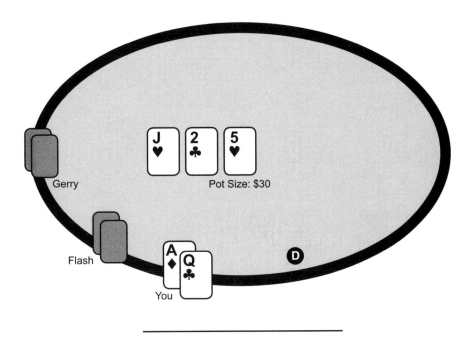

The flop comes J♥ 2♣ 5♥. You check, and, to your surprise, so do your opponents.

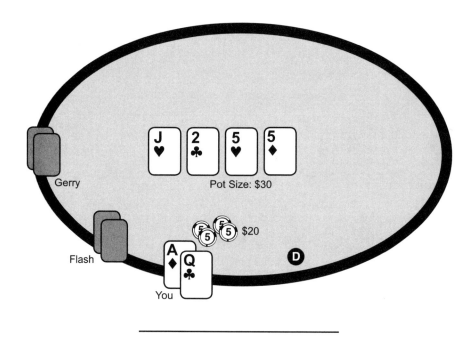

The turn pairs the 5 and it's up to you to act. At this point you think there's an excellent chance that you have the best hand. There is always the possibility that the big blind checked a 2 or a 5 on the flop, or that the under-the-gun caller is slowplaying a monster, but if you do have the best hand, you certainly can't afford to give any free cards.

You bet and both your opponents fold.

Were you to get raised here you would use your knowledge of the player to make a decision about whether to proceed. You'd be more likely to fold if the under-the-gun player was the raiser.

$10-$20 HOLD'EM: TEN-HANDED

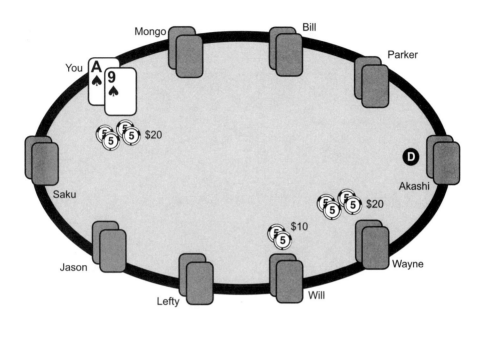

| KEY CONCEPTS |

• Giving a free card to avoid being outplayed
• Continuation bets

You have A-9 suited in middle position and the players acting before you have folded. You raise and all the players fold to the small blind, who calls. The big blind folds.

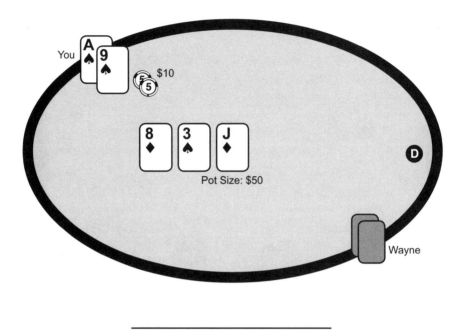

The flop comes 8♦ 3♠ J♦. Your opponent checks, and, as you usually do heads-up if you've raised before the flop, you bet even though the flop hasn't helped you.

Your opponent calls.

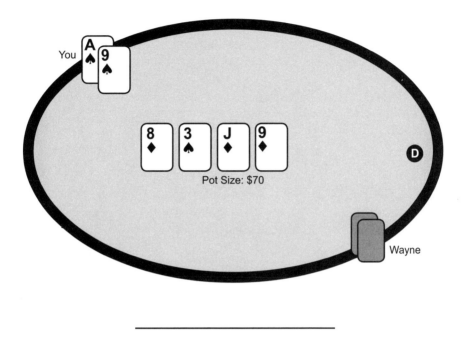

The turn brings the 9♦. This is a dangerous card for you. Although it makes you a pair of 9s with an ace kicker, which might just be the best hand, you know your opponent is a very tricky player and that at this point he has at worst a strong draw. Again, Wayne checks. You feel pretty sure that if you bet, he is going to raise you and you're not interested in putting in three more bets with your pair of 9s. On the other hand, you feel confident that if you check you will get another bet out of him on the end if you do indeed have the best hand. If you check now and he ends up at the river with a busted draw, you are sure that he will bluff on the end and you will call. If Wayne checks you will bet your 9s for value unless the board makes your hand look hopeless.

The majority of the time you would bet here and fold if raised, but this time you decide to check and hope to make a bet on the end if you have the best hand. Usually this would be a very bad check, because there are just too many cards that can fall to beat your hand if you indeed have the best hand on the turn.

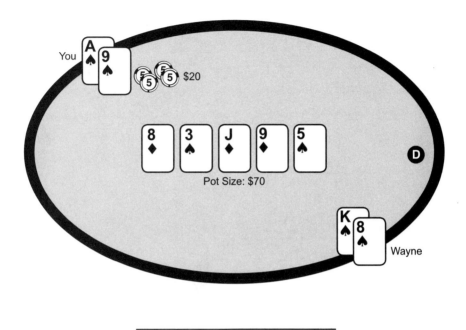

The river brings the 5♠, which is probably a blank, and Wayne checks to you. You bet your 9s for value.

As you hoped, Wayne calls with a worse hand.

$10-$20 HOLD'EM: TEN-HANDED

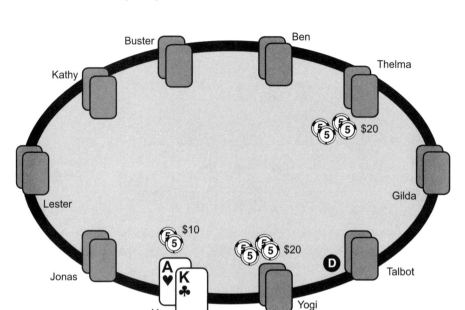

KEY CONCEPTS

• Waiting until the flop to put in extra bets
• Big blind play
• Betting overcards for value
• Not giving free cards

In this example, you have A-K offsuit in the big blind. Everybody folds to the player in position No. 8 and she raises. The cutoff and the button fold and the small blind calls the raise. Now it is up to you. I suggest you flat-call most of the time in this spot, because then you keep the strength of your hand a secret until you decide to reveal it. You get the advantage of seeing what your opponents do on the flop and can almost always get a raise or check-raise in if you want to. You can also bet out and sometimes get three bets on the flop if you decide to take that route. You just call.

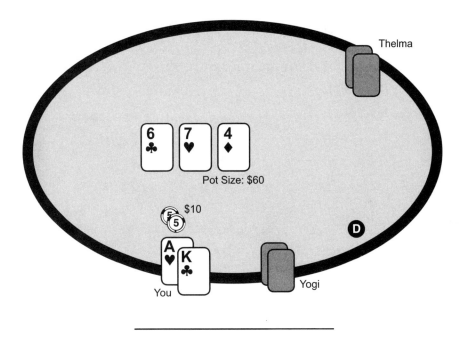

The flop comes 6-7-4 rainbow and the small blind checks to you. You think there is a very good chance that you have the best hand at this point. If you check, the late-position raiser will probably bet and there is a decent chance that the small blind will call. Then you won't have any idea where you stand. Also, you will then be playing against two players and not have control of the pot. The pot will be bigger and so it will be more likely they will want to go to the end. Your best chance to win the pot or at least get it heads-up is to bet out on the flop. It is fairly likely that you could have a piece of this flop since you're in the big blind and would call with many hands that would fit this flop. Your hand also beats any no-pair hand, including all draws.

If you get raised by Thelma and the small blind folds, you will probably play your hand for the best hand and reraise. If the player in late position folds and the small blind calls, you will proceed cautiously. If the player in late position folds and the small blind raises, you will take off one card and consider folding if he bets again on the turn, unless you hit an ace or a king.

You bet out.

Both players fold and you win the pot. This is the result that you were looking for.

$10-$20 HOLD'EM: NINE-HANDED

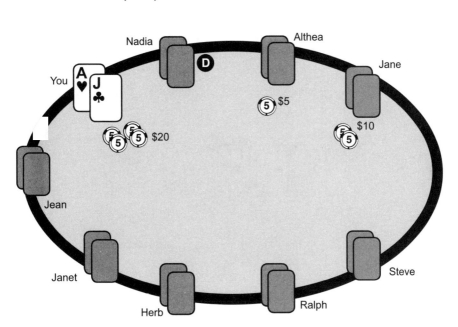

KEY CONCEPTS

- Checking for maximum value
- Continuation bets on the flop

Everybody folds to you in the cutoff and you have A-J offsuit, a very strong hand for this position. You raise thinking that you will be pleased to win only the blinds but, if they call, you're happy to have more money in the pot as you think you probably have the best hand.

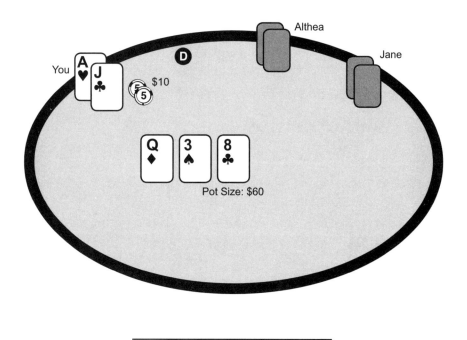

Both the blinds call your preflop raise and the flop comes Q-3-8 rainbow. Although it hasn't helped you, there is no reason to think it helped your opponents either. With a flop like this, unless your opponents already have a pair or have made a pair on the flop, a bet will often win the pot. That's because a lot of the hands they may have called your preflop raise with will have no reason to continue. Hands like A-10, K-J, K-10, and any other ace with a kicker other than a queen, 8, or 3 will likely fold if you bet. There also isn't a flush draw out there. Since they both check to you and you have already shown strength, you bet.

If the flop had come with both a king and a queen, you'd probably check behind them because it would be much less likely that you could take the pot with a bet on the flop so you'd want to take the free card to try to make your straight or catch an ace.

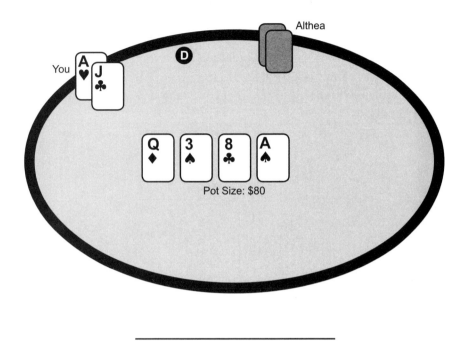

The small blind calls your bet and the big blind folds. The turn brings the A♠, which is an excellent card for you. Your opponent checks to you. Most players would bet here, but you check to try for maximum value.

Your reasoning is as follows. If your opponent has an ace in her hand, you probably lose nothing by checking, because she will surely bet the river, after which you can raise and she will probably call your raise. If she has a small pair or a 3 or an 8, your bet here would probably make her fold her hand and you would get nothing further from the hand. Because so many people try to steal the blinds from late position when everyone has folded to them, it is very possible that you don't have much of a hand. If she has a small piece of the board, your check on the turn will entice her to call any bet you make on the river. Besides the two backdoor draws out there, the only other hands that have a chance to beat you that you are giving a free card to are ones that have either a small piece of the board or pocket pairs.

The chance of Althea having the backdoor draw is rather remote, so you are not going to worry too much about that. The most likely hand for her to have is a pocket pair, ace, 8, or 3. If she has a pocket pair she is drawing to two outs. If she has an 8 or a 3 she is drawing to five outs.

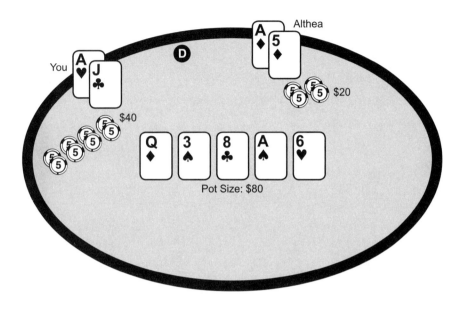

The last card is the 6♥ and your opponent bets out. As you planned, you raise. Against most players, you win the maximum on the hand by playing it this way. Even if Althea had as little as K-10, you will win an extra bet by playing the hand this way, since she will probably check and call with a hand as weak as that after you checked the turn.

Because your opponent calls the raise on the river, you win the same amount you would have if you had bet the turn. She would have checked and called on the river in that case. But the advantage of this play is that you would have gotten one more bet from a weak hand than you would have had you bet the turn because a no-pair hand that might call on the river would fold on the turn.

$10-$20 HOLD'EM: TEN-HANDED

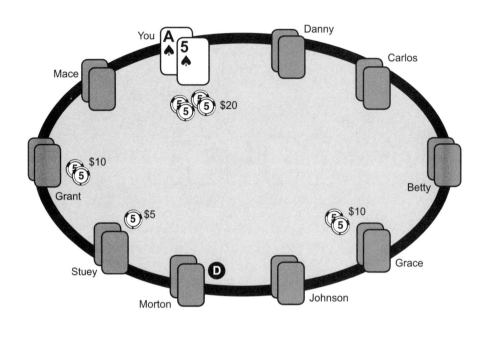

- Aggressive play when there is an extra blind in the pot
- Continuation bets

Here's a rare situation in which you can play ace-small suited in very early position. The reason you are playing it here is because there is an extra blind in the pot and you are playing in a very tight game. The extra blind means there is 40 percent more money to shoot for. You're not the only player aware of this extra money, which is why you've decided to raise with the type of hand that you have. You know there is a good chance that other players will be attracted by the extra money and will suspect that you're trying to steal the blinds. Therefore you're making this play with a hand that plays very well in a multiway pot. Ideally, you'd like everybody to fold so that you can win the blinds, but if a number of players call, you have the right type of hand. The under-the-gun player folds and you come in for a raise with A♠ 5♠.

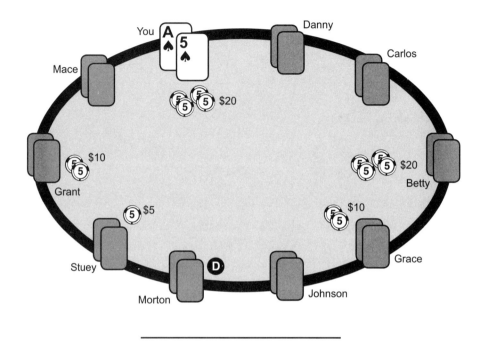

You end up getting one caller behind you and all the blinds fold.

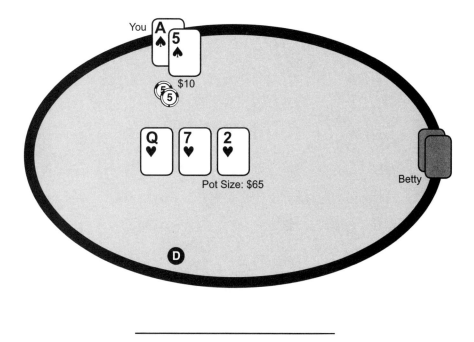

Although Q♥ 7♥ 2♥ is a terrible flop for you, it doesn't necessarily have to have helped your opponent. There's far too much money in there for you not to put up a fight. Your best chance to win the hand is to bet this flop. Your second-best chance to win the hand is to check-raise.

You bet out and the lone caller folds.

$10-$20 HOLD'EM: EIGHT-HANDED

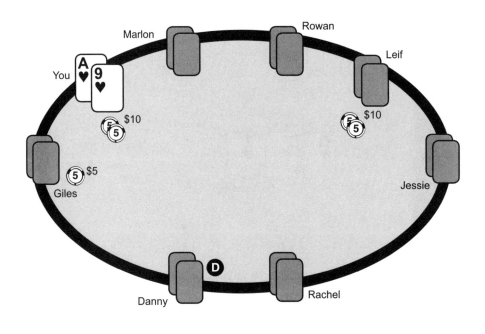

KEY CONCEPTS

- Playing a weak ace from the big blind
- Betting a marginal hand to avoid giving a free card

You have a A♥ 9♥, a good hand in the big blind. There is one limper in position No. 5 and all the other players fold to you. Although there is a good chance that you have the best hand, there is no reason for you to raise. If you want, you will probably be able to get a check-raise later. Also, it is quite likely that the flop will miss your hand completely, which will put you in a difficult position if you raise now and then are first to act. This is not the type of hand that you are completely comfortable playing to the end if you miss the flop. If you had A-K, you would feel a lot more comfortable betting it as the best hand all the way even if you didn't pair, so you would be more inclined to raise preflop with it. You check.

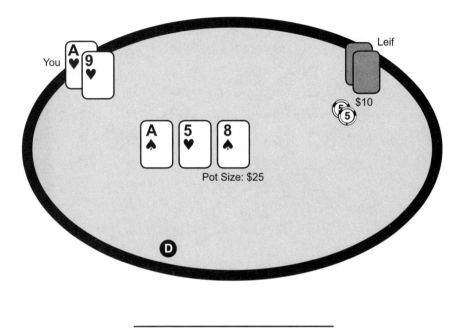

The flop comes A♠ 5♥ 8♠. Although you flop aces, you're not sure where you're at, so you check, expecting your opponent to bet regardless of what hand he has.

He bets and you call. About half the time you would probably check-raise here, but this time you decide to call and see what comes on the turn before determining how to play the later streets.

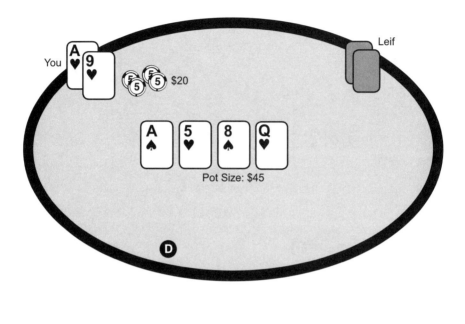

The turn brings the Q♥. You bet and take the pot. Why did you bet? Well, first of all, even when you called on the flop, you thought there was a good chance that you had the best hand. There are a couple of reasons you waited until the turn to bet. The first reason is that unless you are drawing only to the flush, you will probably not get raised. When you bet out on the turn, it looks very much like you might have made two pair. Unless your opponent also has two pair or perhaps a set, it is very unlikely that he will raise you. Even if he has a hand like A-K, there is a good chance that he will just call. If you do get raised in this spot, you will believe that you are beaten, but you probably still have nine hearts and possibly three 9s to catch to win the pot.

So the first reason that you bet out is because you were going to call anyway, and it is unlikely that you'll be getting raised by A-K,

A-J, or A-10. The second reason that you bet out is that you do not want to give a free card if you have the best hand. When the queen falls, you certainly do not want to give a free card to a hand like K-J, K-10, J-10, 10-9, or a spade draw.

As it turns out, your opponent must have been way behind, because he folds.

$10-$20 HOLD'EM: NINE-HANDED

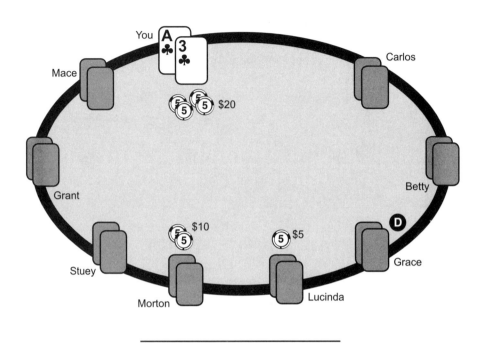

KEY CONCEPTS

• Aggressive play and continuation bets in a tight game

You are in a very tight game. Sometimes in extremely tight games a lot of your profit comes from stealing the blinds. That's why you are raising here with a hand that generally does not warrant a raise. When you make a play like this, your best result in the long run is to simply win the blinds.

As you suspected, all the other players fold, but the big blind does call your raise.

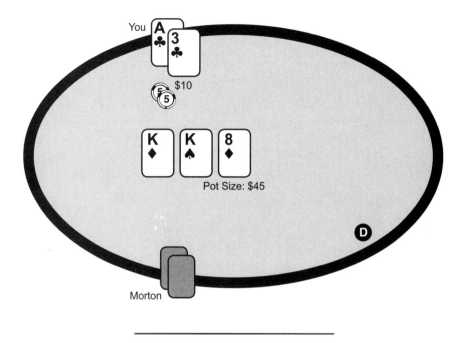

The flop comes K♦ K♠ 8♦ and the big blind checks to you. You bet, and the big blind folds. Almost regardless of what came, you were intending to bet the flop if the big blind checked to you. Because you had shown strength before the flop, you were able to win this hand.

The main point here is that you adjusted your play away from normal ring game strategy because of the type of game you were in. Normally you would have either folded your ace-small suited or just limped in. Because you thought there was a good chance that you could win the blinds in this particular game by playing it very strongly, you adjusted your basic strategy and played in a manner more conducive to the game.

SECTION

OVERVIEW

The main focus of many of the hands in this section is getting maximum value and the many different ways you can accomplish that. We discuss some of the advantages of occasionally slowplaying high pairs before the flop from the blinds, both for deception and to get maximum value with minimum risk. Some of the example hands point out situations in which check-raising is preferable to leading out, while others describe situations in which leading out with a bet or leading into a raiser is the best way to go.

We also discuss some marginal situations and how to value-bet them depending upon your read of your opponents. We'll also look at aggressive play on the flop, taking control of a hand, and playing top pair strongly.

$10-$20 HOLD'EM: NINE-HANDED

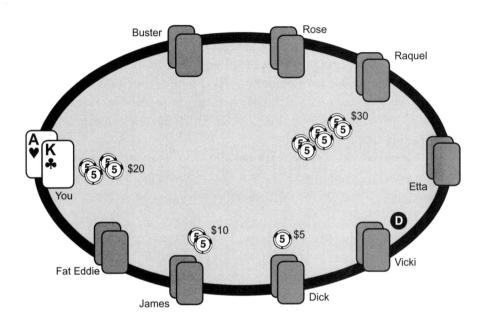

KEY CONCEPTS

- Leading into strength to get maximum value
- Slowplaying
- Allowing your opponents to bet for you

This example shows how to get maximum value by playing a hand in a somewhat unconventional manner. You have A♥ K♣ in early position and raise. You get reraised from late position. Everybody folds to the big blind, who calls. It is now up to you.

Although some people cap it in this situation, I think that is not usually a good play. There is a good chance that you don't have the best hand. If you just call and the flop helps you, you will almost surely be able to get in a raise or a check-raise. If you miss completely, you will be able to get away with minimum loss. You just call as well.

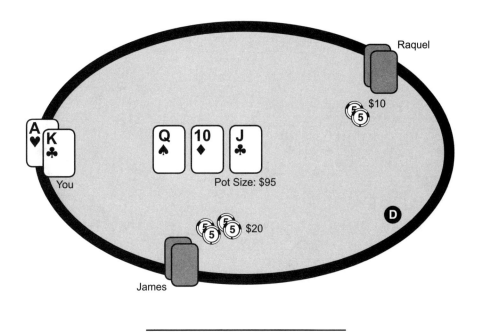

You flop a monster, so now you have to think about how you can get the most out of the hand. It is fairly obvious that if someone has A-K, he has flopped the nuts, and you don't want your opponents to suspect you have that hand. The big blind checks, as do you, and the late-position reraiser bets. The big blind check-raises. It's now up to you.

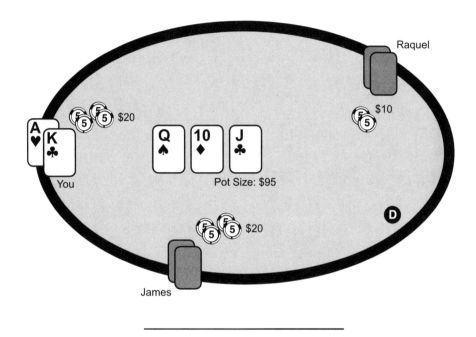

You know you're up against two players who have a hand, but you still think you are the only one with a nut straight. You decide to flat-call here, rather than reveal the strength of your hand just yet. You'll make your decision about how to play it on the turn depending on a number of different factors. The first is whether the late-position player reraises here. The second is what comes on the turn. The third is how the big blind plays his hand on the turn.

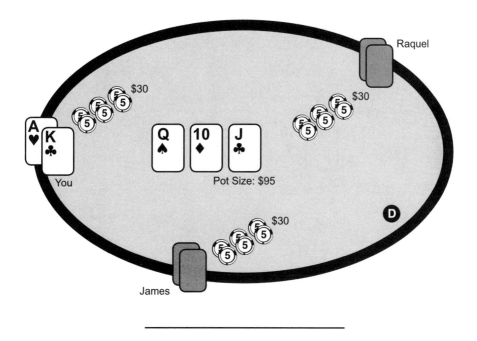

The late-position player reraises, the big blind calls, and you call. There is no reason for you to cap it here, as that would just blow your whole strategy.

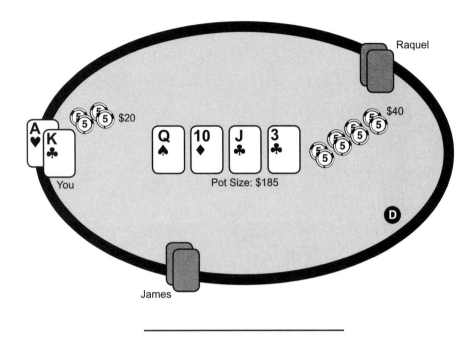

The turn brings the 3♣, certainly a complete blank for this situation, and the big blind checks. You think there is a good chance that the big blind has either two pair or a pair with a straight draw. You wouldn't mind knocking him out of the hand. If he has a smaller straight or the same hand as you do, nothing you do will get him out of the hand. You decide to throw in a confusing bet, hoping to get raised by the late-position player.

You bet out and, sure enough, the late-position player raises you.

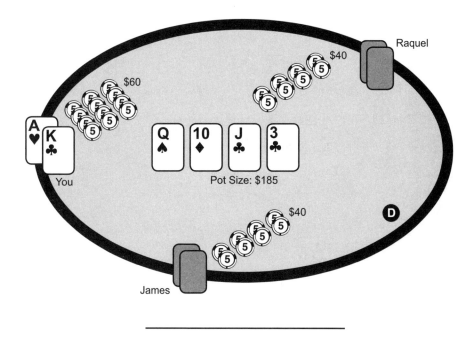

The big blind calls the raise, and now you go for maximum value by reraising. Although it's likely both of them have finally figured out what you have, they have so much money invested in the pot that it's unlikely they'll fold.

They both call your reraise.

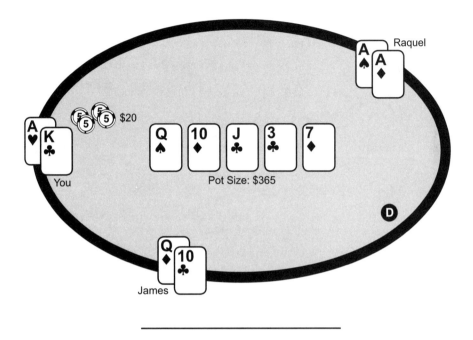

The river brings the 7♦, another complete blank. The big blind checks and you bet, trying to get at least one last bet from each player.

Partially because of the size of the pot, both players call and you win a huge pot, getting maximum value.

$10-$20 HOLD'EM: SEVEN-HANDED

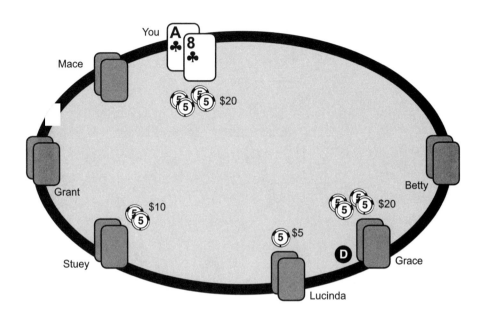

KEY CONCEPTS

- Playing top pair strongly
- Reading players
- Betting for value

You're in a somewhat short-handed game, so you loosen up your starting requirements and raise coming in with A-8 suited in position No. 5. You're hoping the last two players fold, but the player on the button calls your raise, as does the big blind.

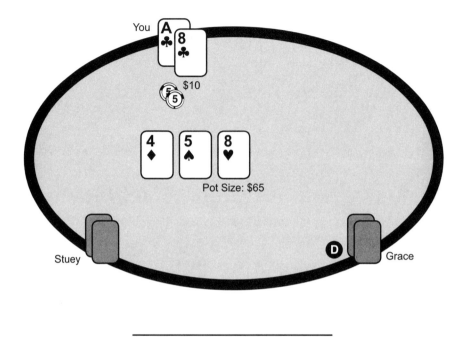

The flop comes 4-5-8 rainbow, a pretty good flop for you. The big blind checks and you bet. Both players call.

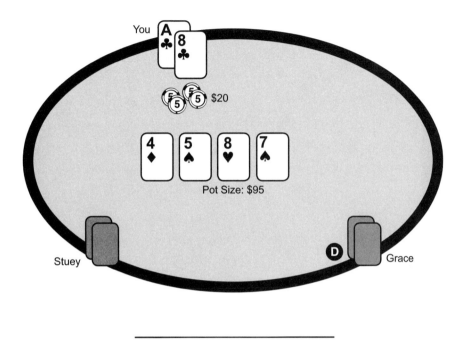

The turn brings the 7♠, and the big blind checks to you. This is by no means a good card for you, but the player you are most worried about with a board like this is Stuey and he has checked to you. Although it's possible that the player on the button might have a straight or two pair, it's much more likely that she has two high cards. Grace called your raise before the flop but did not reraise you. That's a strong indication that she doesn't have a pair in the hole. With the flop like this, if she had any piece of the board she probably would've raised you on the flop in an attempt to knock the big blind out and get heads-up with you. If Grace had a hand like 4-5, 5-6, 6-8, or 7-8, she also probably would've raised you on the flop. You bet, hoping that both of the players fold. If you get raised or check-raised you'll just have to make a value judgment based on your knowledge of the players. You certainly can't afford to check here because there are too many cards that could fall on the river to beat you.

The player on the button calls and the small blind folds. This is an excellent result for you.

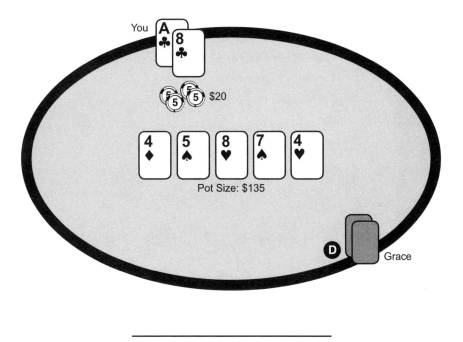

The river pairs the board and there's no reason to believe that this card helped your opponent. You still feel strongly that you have the best hand, but the question is how do you make the most money on this final street. Many times, if you think your opponent has been drawing and has missed, you will check on the river and give her a chance to bluff. In this particular situation you think it is very unlikely that your opponent will try to bluff, because you played the hand so strongly that it's fairly obvious that you have something.

If you had nothing, or a hand like A-K, you almost surely would not have bet on the turn against two players with such a dangerous board. Since you don't think your opponent will bluff and you don't think she has a piece of this board, you bet, hoping she has enough to call you. Your opponent folds.

This hand is a good example of when not to miss a value bet

due to a scary board. Many players would look at this board and automatically check the river because of all the possibilities for hands stronger than 8s and 4s with an ace kicker. Part of your job as an expert player is to evaluate whether the obvious conclusion is the best by putting together all the pieces to the puzzle.

$10-$20 HOLD'EM: TEN-HANDED

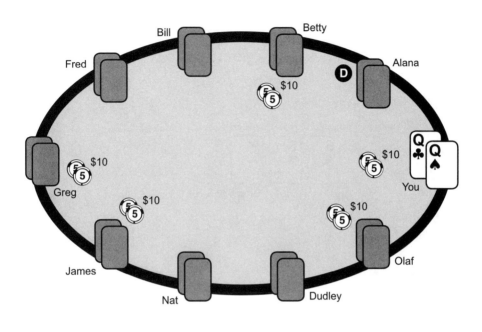

■ KEY CONCEPTS

- Gaining value through defensive play
- Slow-playing a high pair before the flop

You have a pair of queens in the small blind. There are three callers in, besides the big blind. There are two ways to play this hand. You can raise and bet all the way through unless you feel sure you're beat, or you can take a more conservative approach. In this hand, you decide to just call and see what develops on the flop. The big blind calls and now it is a five-way unraised pot.

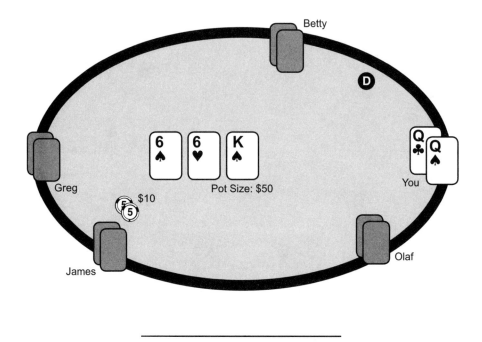

The flop is 6♠ 6♥ K♠. A flop like this is either very good or very bad for you. Although you think there is a good chance that you have the best hand, you check to see what develops, and Olaf checks behind you. Betting out and playing your hand for the best hand would be a reasonable alternative as well.

James bets and the two original callers before you fold. You decide to call and see what the big blind does. You're getting 6 to 1 on a hand that probably has at least a 40 percent chance of being the best.

The big blind folds. Had the big blind raised here, depending on what type of player he was, you would have considered folding.

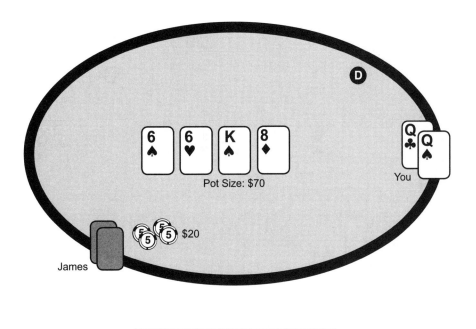

The turn brings the 8♦. You decide to let James continue to bet the hand. He bets again. If he is an extremely conservative player, you will usually fold here. Otherwise, you often will check and call all the way. There is a decent possibility that he has either a medium pair in the hole or a spade draw. Your hand is simply too good to throw away except against very tight players. Occasionally you will check-raise on the turn if you think he is betting a draw or a smaller pair. You could also bet out on the turn because there is little chance you will get raised since your opponent should be concerned that you might have a 6 since you just called from the small blind.

This time you simply call.

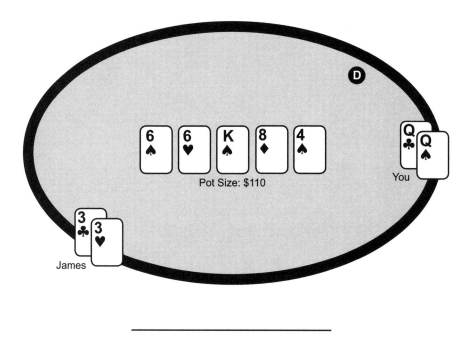

The river brings a spade. You check and so does your opponent. You win.

Another way to play the river would be for you to bet here planning to fold if he raises. The reason you might do this is to get value from any pair smaller than yours that might check, but would call if you bet. A king with a good kicker would likely not raise you but would probably bet if you check, which you would call, so you lose nothing extra by betting into that hand. A king with a bad kicker may well check here, but would call you if you bet, so in that case you would lose an extra bet by betting out on the end.

$15-$30 HOLD'EM: TEN-HANDED

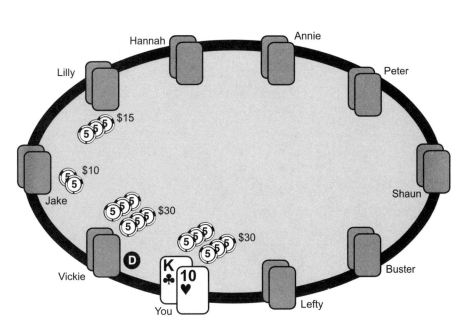

KEY CONCEPTS

• Checking for maximum value

You are in the cutoff and everyone has folded to you. You have K♣ 10♥. You would usually raise here with any average hand or better in an attempt to steal the blinds.

You raise, the player on the button calls and the two blinds fold. That is not a bad result for you, but you will have to be cautious on the flop because you don't have position and may well have the worst hand.

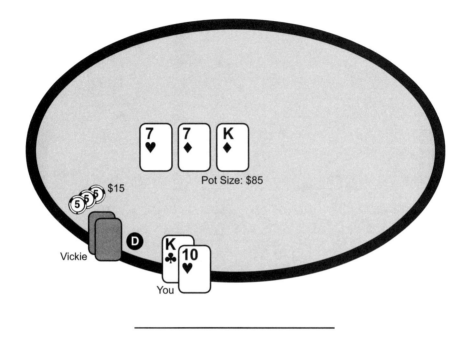

The flop comes 7♥ 7♦ K♦ and is quite a good flop for you. Unless your opponent has a king with a better kicker than yours or a 7, you almost certainly have the best hand. You know your opponent is aware that you would have raised preflop in this situation with almost any two cards, so you decide to take advantage of that fact. You want Vickie to think that you have missed the flop and that she can take the pot away from you. You're not worried about giving a free card because there isn't much she could be drawing to. You're against only one opponent and the only draw on the board is a flush draw.

You check your kings.

Vickie bets and you simply call. You're hoping to get a check-raise in on the turn.

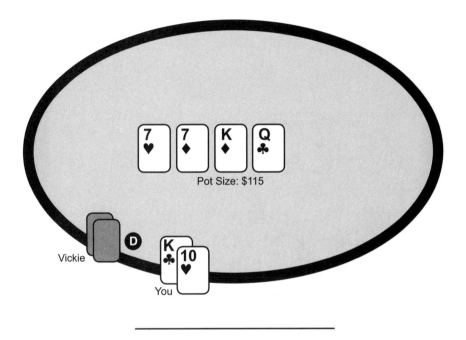

The Q♣ on the turn is a decent card for you. It's likely to have given your opponent at least a draw if not a pair of queens. You're glad it's not an ace as that would be the worst card for you. On the other hand, if Vickie had a worse king than yours, she has now caught up.

You were intending to try for a check-raise on this street. If your opponent has a hand like A-J, A-10, or J-10, she might be inclined to take a free card now. Even so, you gamble and check to her.

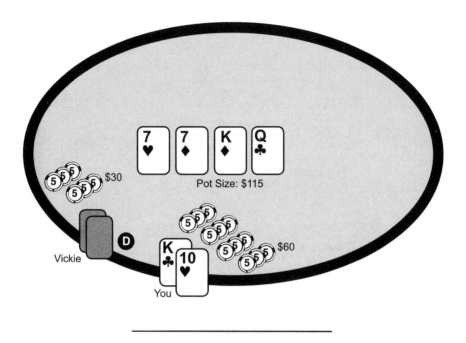

Vickie bets and you check-raise. You are quite confident that you have the best hand and expect a call with as little as a gutshot straight draw. She calls your check-raise.

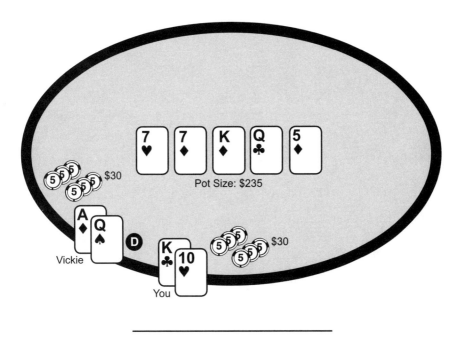

Although the 5♦ on the river completes the flush, you are not concerned about that and bet your hand for value.

Your opponent calls your bet and you win likely the maximum you could have on this hand.

$10-$20 HOLD'EM: SEVEN-HANDED

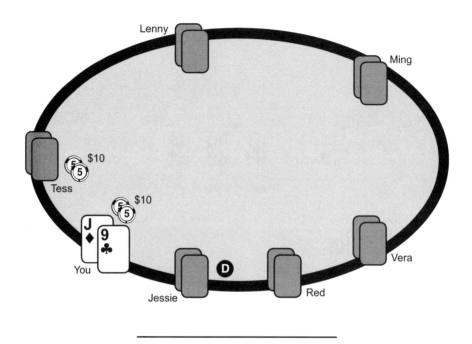

![KEY CONCEPTS]

KEY CONCEPTS

- Small blind play
- Getting maximum value

You are in the small blind and everyone has folded to you. You have J♦ 9♣. Your hand is too good to fold, but doesn't deserve a raise unless you are making a play. Many players routinely try to steal in this situation. Generally speaking, that is not a good idea. Your opponent has position on you, knows that many people try to steal here, and will be getting 3 to 1 on her call. You just call and the big blind checks.

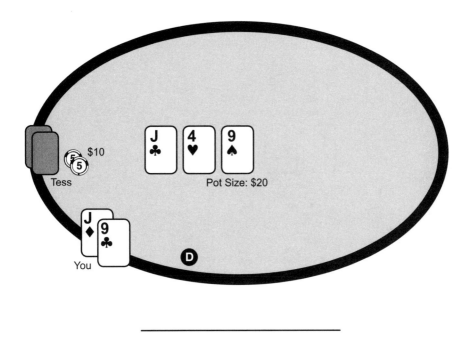

You flop a monster, J♣ 9♠ 4♥ but have to decide how to get the most out of it. You first think about how your opponent plays. You decide to check-raise since your opponent is a bit aggressive and you have shown weakness by just calling before the flop.

You check, and your opponent bets. Now you check-raise. Your opponent calls.

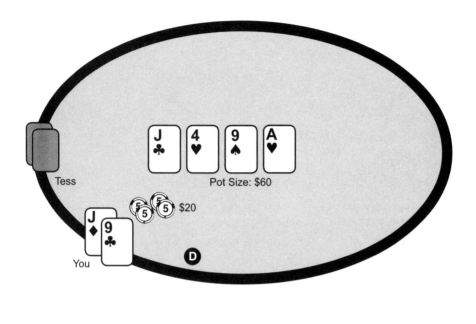

The turn is an ace, but you can't worry about your opponent making two pair. You bet out. Trying for a check-raise here is probably not a good idea, because there is no reason to think the ace hit her. If Tess had an ace, she probably would have raised before the flop.

Your opponent should fold here because there is little that she can beat. Even if she catches a queen, it is the type of card that could make you a stronger hand than she has. She calls anyway. At this point, you have every reason to believe you are ahead.

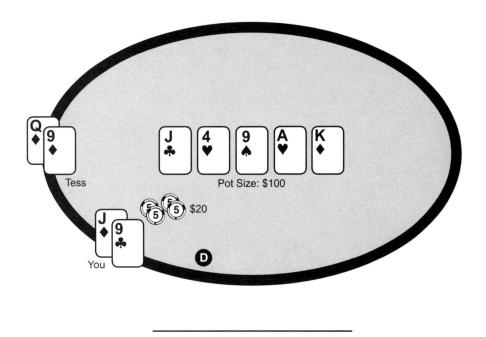

A king comes on the river. It's not an ideal card for you, but you must bet for value unless you think you can induce a bluff. The only draw your opponent could have completed would be Q-10. Her call on the turn indicated she had a piece of the board. A lot of players get stubborn and call one last bet on the end even if they have little chance of winning. This is your opportunity to get that bet. If you are in a situation like this, you shouldn't worry about two pair until you get raised. Just because there are two overcards to your hand is not a reason to check. Even if you get raised on the end, you should still call most of the time because many players use scare cards as an excuse to try to steal the pot.

You bet. Tess should fold, but she calls anyway. This is not a good call because about all that she can beat is a bluff. Also, the pot odds are not very high because it's a heads-up unraised pot. You stack your chips.

$10-$20 HOLD'EM: NINE-HANDED

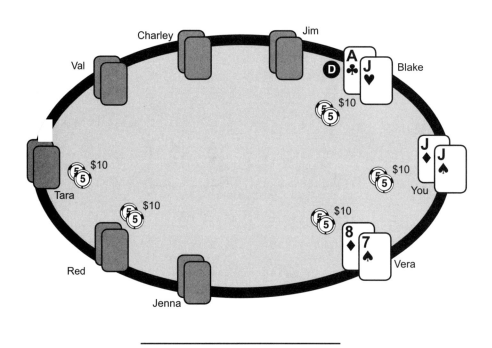

KEY CONCEPTS

- Slow-playing jacks in the small blind
- Aggressive play on the flop
- Getting maximum value
- Check-raising

You have pocket jacks in the small blind. Two players and the button have limped. This example shows a couple of different sophisticated plays. The first is playing it cool with a strong hand in bad position to see what comes and possibly narrowing the field if you like what you see. The second is getting maximum value out of a strong hand. In this situation, raising before the flop will not knock any players out of the pot, and will make the pot so large that it will almost certainly be a multiway pot to the end. For that reason, you decide to just call and see what comes on the flop. The big blind checks behind you. If you feel you're ahead on the flop, you will probably try to check-raise in an attempt to narrow down the field.

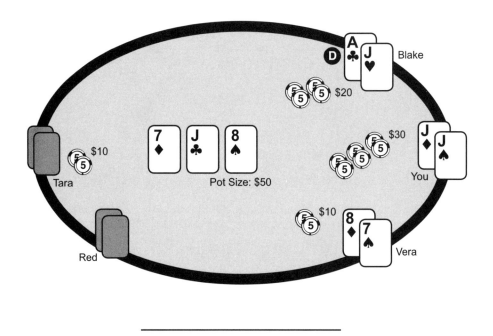

The flop is 7♦ J♣ 8♠, giving you three jacks. You check. Vera bets, Red calls, Tara folds, and Blake, on the button, raises. You can now play this hand to the hilt, expecting to get a lot of action. You make it three bets.

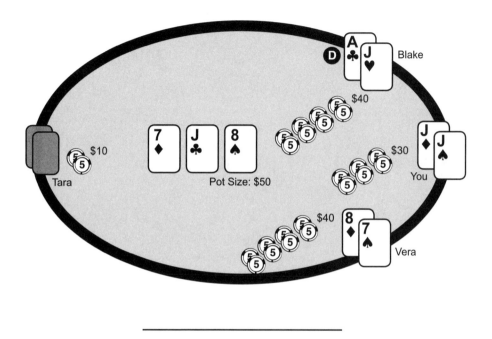

Vera, the big blind, caps it with bottom two pair. Tara folds and Blake calls. You call. We'll see the turn three-handed.

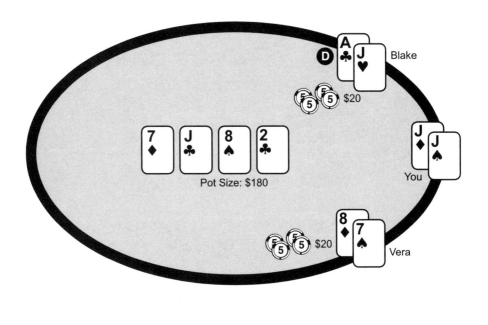

The 2♣ comes on the turn, a card unlikely to have helped anyone. There is a possibility that one of the other players has 9-10, but you're going to play your top set strongly on the turn anyway to see what develops. You check, feeling certain one of the other two players, probably the big blind, will bet. There is a decent chance you are up against a set or two pair and top pair with a good kicker.

The big blind bets, and the button calls.

Now you get that extra value by check-raising. You expect both players to call and there is a chance one of them will reraise. If you get reraised, you will certainly call but against most players you will not raise it again. If you get raised twice, you will still call as you can draw out on a straight if the board pairs and it is also possible someone with a smaller set would cap it. If you have the best hand (likely), you have succeeded in getting maximum value on two streets. Both of the other players call your check-raise.

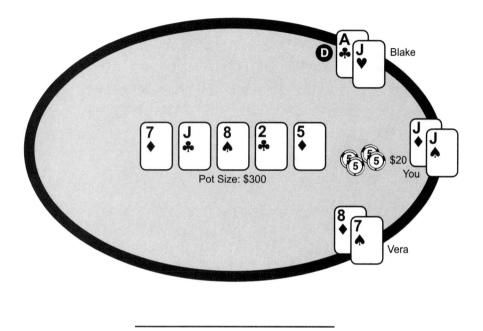

The 5♦ on the river doesn't change anything, so you bet out confident that you have the best hand. Both players call, and you win a large pot.

$15-$30 HOLD'EM: TEN-HANDED

KEY CONCEPTS

- Adjusting for loose-aggressive games
- Reading players
- Reraising to narrow the field
- Playing a marginal hand aggressively

Sometimes you find yourself in a game that is "wild and crazy" with lots of players in every hand. This example is from that type of game. You have A♠ 10♠ in middle position and the first three players have folded. You want as many players in as possible, so you just call, hoping that others will follow.

The player to your left folds, the next player calls, and the player to his left raises. The button and small blind fold, the big blind calls, and it's up to you.

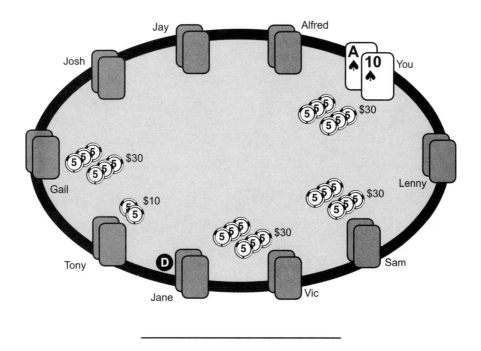

You think there is a good chance that you have the best hand at this point because the raise from the player in late position doesn't mean much in this game. You'd like to see a big pot, so you just call. Actually, in this game, even if you raised, the other players would probably still come. After you call, the player in position No. 8 calls as well, and this is now a four-way pot with nine small bets in it before the flop.

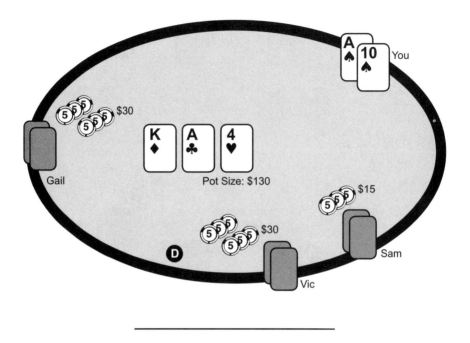

The flop comes K♦ A♣ 4♥ and the big blind checks to you. Although you flopped an ace, you decide to wait and see what happens, so you check as well. The player behind you bets and the late-position raiser raises him. The player in the big blind calls and it's up to you.

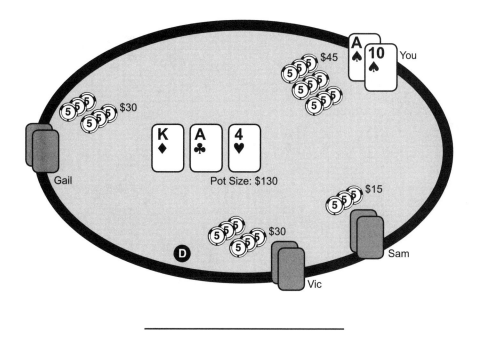

If this was a very tight game, you would probably fold your hand, but, as mentioned, this is a loose-aggressive game. The original raiser had been raising a lot of pots and, also as mentioned, his raise didn't necessarily indicate a strong hand. You think that the player in front of him is aware of this and could well have been betting out hoping to get raised, in an attempt to narrow the field to a heads-up situation. That the blind called the raise doesn't worry you, as you still think you have her beat.

You decide there is a very good chance that you hold the best hand and so you want to put pressure on the original bettor and the blind hand. You also think the original raiser might reraise with a worse hand than yours, which might make the blind hand fold. You further think that Sam knows he might be forced to put in four bets if he calls.

You make it three bets for all those reasons.

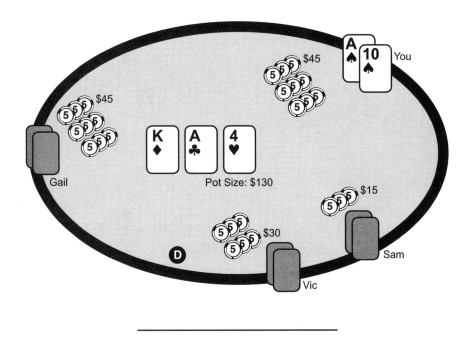

Your plan works a bit differently than you anticipated, since only the big blind calls the third bet, but you did end up in a two-way contest against a hand you think is probably worse than yours.

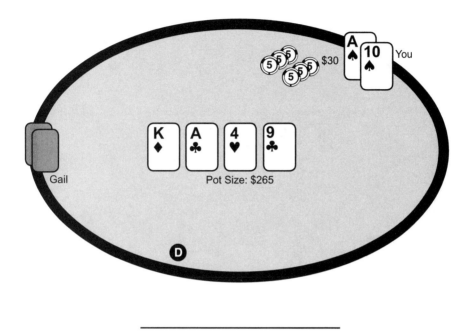

The turn brings the 9♣, a relative blank, and the blind checks to you. You bet, knowing that she might have you beat, but thinking you aren't likely to get raised. If she is on a draw, checking would be a very bad play, and you can always check the end if you so choose. If you checked here and Gail bet the end you would call anyway, so it's better to bet here. She calls.

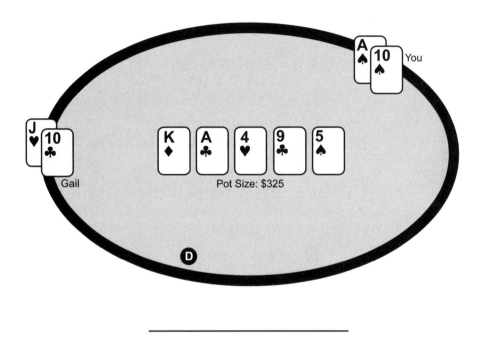

The river brings the 5♠, a card that probably didn't improve Gail's hand and she checks to you. Although you check the end, it's quite possible that a better play would have been to bet your A-10 for value. You put her on a hand with a gutshot straight and maybe a backdoor flush draw, like K-Q, Q-J, J-10, or K-x. You also thought there was a decent chance that she had A-Q, A-J, or the same hand as you did. The only hands that you could beat that were likely to call a river bet were A-8, A-7, A-6, A-3, and A-2. In retrospect, you think the chance that she had a worse ace was big enough that you should have bet the river.

As you can see, though, in this particular situation, it didn't make a difference. Gail would not have called a bet.

$10-$20 HOLD'EM: TEN-HANDED

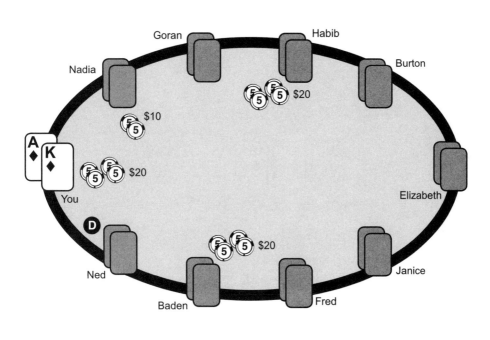

KEY CONCEPTS

- Disguising the strength of your hand
- Check-raising for maximum value
- Taking control of a hand
- Betting for value in marginal situations
- Deciding whether to bet or check on the river
  with a marginal hand

This play should be used only if you know the players you are playing against. You have A♦ K♦ in the small blind. The player in position No. 4 raises and the player in position No. 9 calls.

Even though you feel there is a reasonable chance that you have the best hand, you decide to just call and see what the flop will bring. The big blind folds.

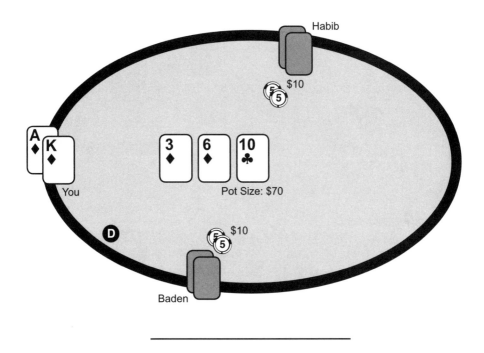

The flop is 3♦ 6♦ 10♣. This is a great flop for you, giving you the nut flush draw with two overcards. It's quite possible that you have 15 outs because any of the nine flush cards, three aces, or three kings could win the pot for you. You decide to go for a check-raise for a couple of reasons. First, you'll get more money in the pot with a great hand. Second, you can take control of the hand and have a chance to win it two ways: either by making the best hand or by forcing your opponents to fold.

Betting out with the hope of getting raised so that you could make it three bets would also be a good way to gain control and possibly win the hand.

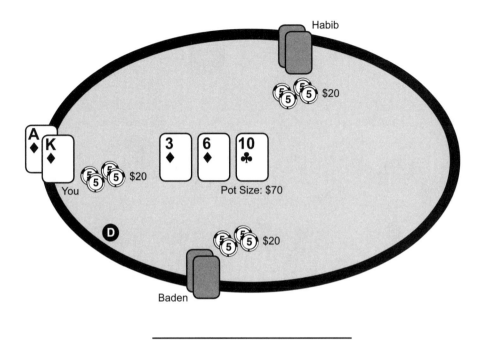

You check, the original opener bets, the player in the cutoff calls, and you check-raise. Both players call. You're thinking there is a decent chance that you have the best hand even without a pair. It's quite likely that both of the other players do not have a pair yet, so even though it may appear that you are semibluffing, you may well be value betting.

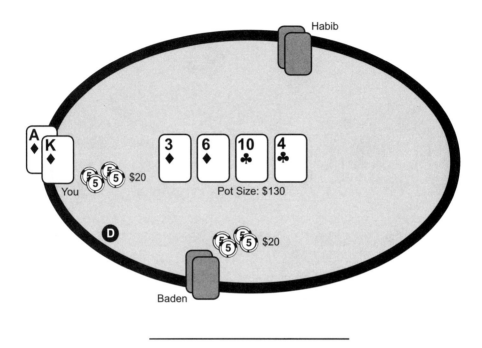

The turn brings a blank, the 4♣, which isn't necessarily the worst thing for you. If you had the best hand on the flop, you almost certainly still do. If you are beaten at this point, you still have a lot of outs. You bet out, and would be happy to win the pot right here. Habib folds but the player in the cutoff calls.

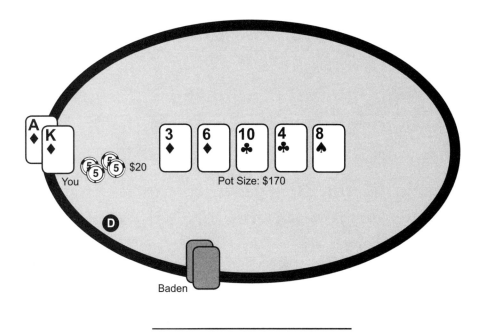

The river brings a relative blank, the 8♠. If Baden was drawing, you have the best hand. If he was calling you down with a worse ace, you have the best hand. If he has a small piece of the board or A-K, you may well be able to win by betting on the end. If you do get called by a better hand, you will eventually make it back in the future because you'll be more likely to be called on the end when you bet for value. You decide to bet out and end up winning the pot when Baden folds.

Another way you could play it is to check on the end hoping to induce a bluff, but much of the time you won't get it because of the action earlier in the hand. You'll miss the extra bet you might get from a stubborn player who will call you with just an ace. You'll also lose to anyone who has a small piece of the board but would have folded to a bet.

The decision whether to bet or check on the end is dependent upon your knowledge of your opponent. If he is likely to bluff but will not call with a hand worse than yours, you should check. If he is unlikely to bluff, but may fold a small pair, you should bet.

SECTION

OVERVIEW

Because you want to be especially careful not to trap yourself, you sometimes have to play defensively. There are ways to maximize your value while playing defensively and this section illustrates some of them.

$10-$20 HOLD'EM: TEN-HANDED

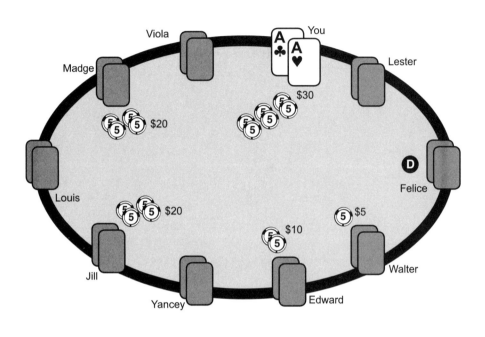

![KEY CONCEPTS]

KEY CONCEPTS

• Defensive play without losing value

Pocket aces can be played many ways. This example shows a rather conservative way that will still usually end up getting you the same number of bets, but may save you a bet when your opponent draws out on you.

Here you have a pair of aces in late position. There is an early-position raise and a middle-position caller. In almost all circumstances, I would recommend reraising with a pair of aces here, for a few reasons. First, you're getting more money in with the best hand. Second, a high pair plays better against fewer opponents, so reraising helps to narrow down the field. In addition, you can get some extra dead money in the pot. You reraise and everybody folds to the initial raiser, who calls, as does the middle-position caller.

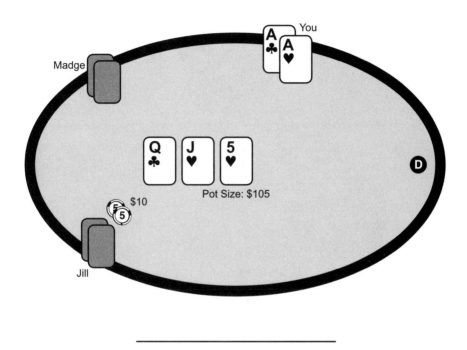

The flop comes Q♣ J♥ 5♥ and the initial raiser bets out. The middle-position player folds, and now it is up to you. When a player raises coming in, gets reraised, calls, and then bets out on the flop, it generally should be taken as a show of strength.

You decide to wait and see what comes on the turn before raising. Although you're pretty sure you have the best hand at this point, you think it is very likely that you will get to raise your opponent on the turn if you so choose. Raising on the turn makes you more money than raising here, and you have the added advantage of seeing what the turn card is.

You call.

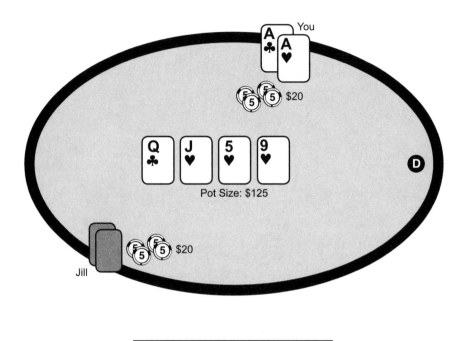

The turn brings the 9♥, a fairly bad card for you. If Jill has K-10, she has now made a straight. If she is drawing to a flush, she has now completed it. On the other hand, you have the ace of hearts in your hand, so you have now gained eight or nine additional outs if she was ahead after the flop.

Many times you would raise here. There's a good chance that you have the best hand, and as mentioned, even if you don't, you have a draw to the nut flush and two more cards that would make three aces. On this particular hand, you decide that if you want to raise on the end you very likely will have that opportunity, and you will probably get called if you do. That way, if a king, 10, queen, or jack comes and you decide not to raise, you may be able to save a bet.

You just flat-call.

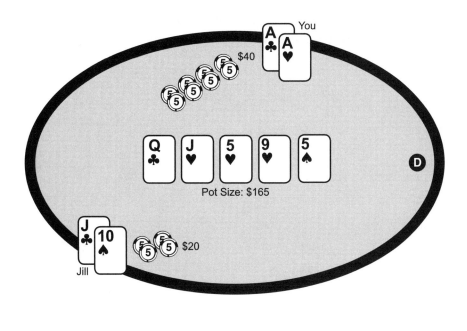

The 5♠ on the river pairs the 5♥. You're not worried that your opponent made three 5s, so this is an excellent card for you. One of the hands that you were concerned about was Q-J. If Jill did indeed have that hand, the pair of 5s on the board would give you a higher two pair.

You were pretty sure all along that you had the best hand, but you feel even more comfortable now. As you can see, you've saved your opportunity to throw in a raise until the last moment, and, provided your opponent calls, you still will make maximum value on this hand.

Jill bets, you raise, she calls, and you win a nice pot.

Although this is a fairly conservative way to play this hand, you can see that you still got as much value as you'd get out of the hand playing it any other way. Occasionally, playing a strong hand this way has the added advantage of getting you some free cards on future hands. If your opponents know that you may sometimes just call them to the end and then raise with a very strong hand, they will be inclined to sometimes give you free cards instead of betting at you.

$10-$20 HOLD'EM: EIGHT-HANDED

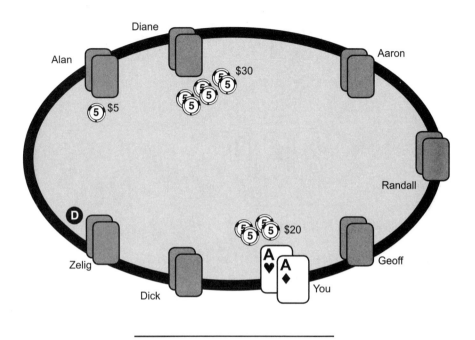

![KEY CONCEPTS]
KEY CONCEPTS

• Saving bets

You are in late position with a pair of aces and the first three players fold to you. You raise and everybody folds except the big blind, who is a very conservative player. She reraises you.

Although you know you have the best hand, you decide to keep it a secret and just call.

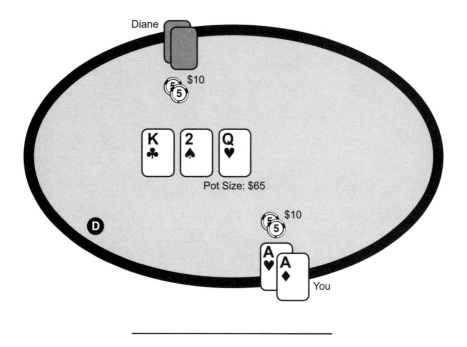

The flop comes K♣ 2♠ Q♥. This is not an ideal flop for you. If Diane has pocket kings or queens, she now has you drawing to two cards. If she has K-Q, you are in almost as bad shape. On the other hand, if Diane has any pair jacks or below, you are in great shape. If she has A-K, K-J, or any worse hand you're also in great shape. You decide you will have the opportunity to raise on the turn if you so choose, so you just flat-call on the flop.

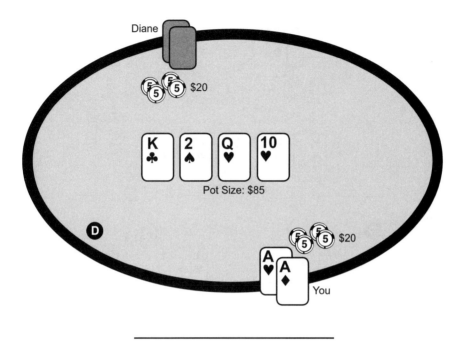

The 10♥ is a very bad card for you. Some hands that your opponent might likely have been playing that would put you in terrible shape are pocket kings, pocket queens, pocket 10s, A-J, and K-Q. Since Diane bet into you again, it's unlikely that she has a pair of 9s or worse. The only two likely hands for her to have that would make you a solid favorite are A-K and pocket jacks. (Although you would be in good shape if she held K-J, it is unlikely that she would have reraised you before the flop with that hand.)

Had the turn come any card other than a king, jack, or 10, you were intending to raise. But this card slows you down. You just call her bet.

By the way, if she had checked here, you would have bet.

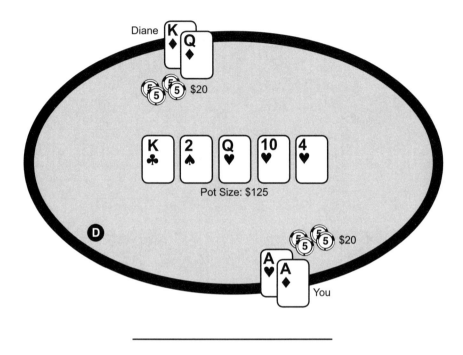

The river brings the 4♥. Although this is a relative blank, it does complete the backdoor flush draw. Along with all the reasons mentioned in the discussion of the turn, that is one more reason to flat-call if Diane bets.

She bets and you call. You end up losing the minimum on this hand.

Had Diane checked the river, you would have bet for value.

$10-$20 HOLD'EM: EIGHT-HANDED

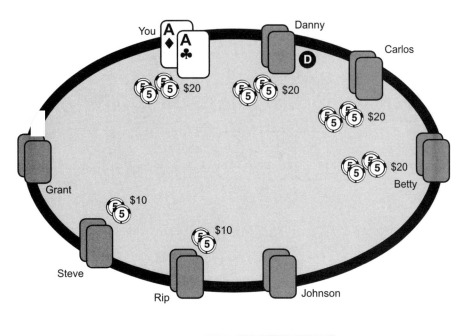

KEY CONCEPTS

• Defensive play based on knowledge of your opponents

This example shows playing pocket aces in a rather unconventional fashion. You raise two limpers in middle position and get a number of callers. Six players see the flop.

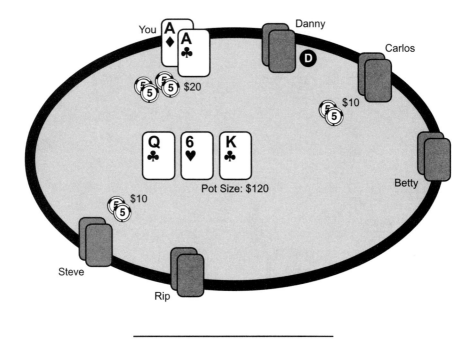

The flop comes Q♣ 6♥ K♣ and the small blind bets out. The next two players fold and Steve, in position No. 5 calls. You raise. Both players call.

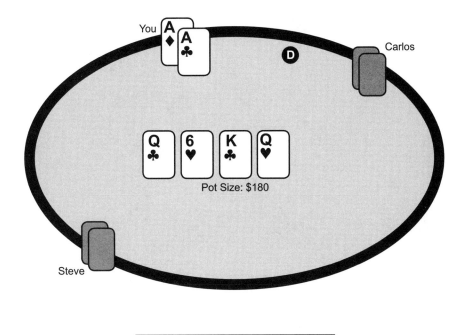

The turn pairs the queens. Although both players check to you, you smell a rat and check behind them. Most of the time you should not check in this situation because this is a very dangerous board to give free cards with. The reason you check here, though, is because you know the players and you have a strong feeling that you are being set up for a check-raise.

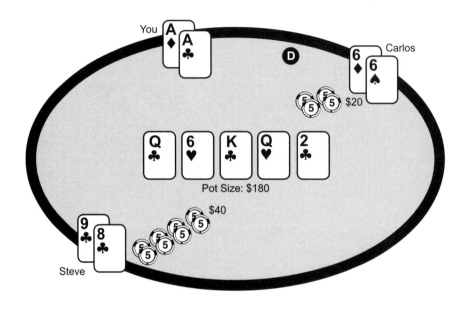

The last card completes the flush draw and the small blind bets out. The middle-position player raises, which makes it an easy fold for you. Through some unconventional defensive play, you end up losing the absolute minimum on this hand. I just want to reiterate that you would very rarely check a pair of aces on the turn in a situation like the one shown, but you used your knowledge of the players and your gut feel to make the right play. Don't get into the habit of checking a hand like this on the turn when there are so many draws out there, because in the long run you will be giving way too many free cards. I just want to illustrate that if you really know your players and have a very strong feeling about what they're planning, you can sometimes save some bets or make some extra bets.

SECTION

OVERVIEW

This is a comprehensive section and it includes a large number of concepts. As in all sections, the importance of reading the players and getting maximum value is covered. We show some ways that aggressive play can help you take control of a hand and illustrate such concepts as playing marginal hands strongly, playing middle pairs for the best hand, and putting pressure on opponents you think are drawing when you have a mediocre made hand. We'll also go over playing overpairs aggressively.

The ability to isolate opponents is essential. We'll discuss a number of different situations in which this comes into play. Often you want to isolate a hand you suspect is weaker than yours. You may also wish to isolate aggressive players who could be holding any two cards. Sometimes you suspect a player is on a complete bluff but you think you may not have another player in the pot beaten, so you want to get heads-up with the bluffer. Other times you may have a hand, like A-J offsuit, that plays better against one opponent than it does in a multiway pot. You may have the opportunity to three-bet the pot to narrow down the field or you may have to resort to a check-raise to knock out the players who are between the bettor and you.

We'll also go into such difficult concepts as folding strong hands, being raised on the turn after you check-raised the flop, and avoiding being bluffed out. Common key concepts like free cards, semibluffing, continuation bets, and mixing up your play are also illustrated.

$10-$20 HOLD'EM: TEN-HANDED

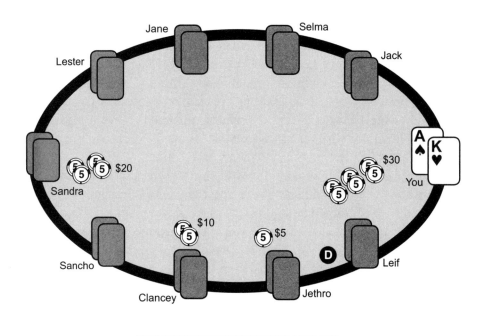

KEY CONCEPTS

- Reraising to isolate with a hand that plays well heads-up
- Reading players
- Value betting
- Dealing with scare cards

Here is a situation that comes up frequently. Somebody has raised from early position and you are in late position with A-K. Unless the player is supertight, you should almost always reraise in this situation. There are a few reasons that I make this recommendation. The first is to take control of the pot. The second is that A-K generally plays better in a heads-up situation. The third and possibly most important is that by reraising, you will most likely knock out the two blinds, which will put three-fourths of a big bet of dead money in the pot.

You three-bet it, the two blinds fold, and the original raiser calls.

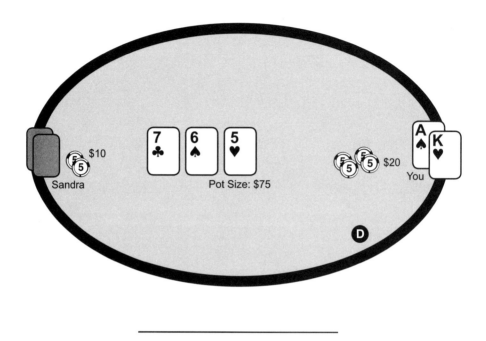

The flop comes 7-6-5 rainbow. This is a bad flop for you, and your opponent bets out. Normally, you would proceed with caution, but you know Sandra to be a very aggressive player who often tries to steal the pot. So you have to consider what type of hand this player might be holding. If she had a high pair, you're pretty sure, knowing her aggressive nature, she would have reraised you before the flop. You also don't think that Sandra has flopped a set, because you think she would have gone for a check-raise if that was the case. It is possible that she has a middle pair, say 8s through jacks.

She also knows you to be a fairly aggressive player, so in her mind it's not unlikely that you might be holding a hand like A-K. Taking into consideration all the factors, you think it is much more likely that she has a hand like A-K, A-Q, A-J, A-10, K-Q, K-J, Q-J, or A-8 suited, and is trying to push you out of the pot. You think there is a very good chance that she believes she can win the pot by being aggressive, provided an ace or a king doesn't fall.

You raise Sandra because you think there is an excellent likelihood that you have the best hand. She calls.

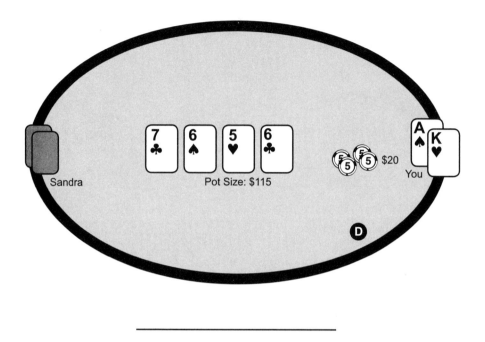

The turn brings the 6♣, which improves your situation if your reasoning is correct. Sandra checks, and you bet your A-K for value.

She check-raises you. Now you have to rethink where you stand. As mentioned earlier, Sandra is a very aggressive player and you need to be careful that she does not take the pot away from you. You feel confident that your initial line of reasoning was sound. You've seen this player try to steal many pots with draws, particularly in heads-up situations. The second 6 might be viewed as a scare card by many players, but in this situation there is no reason to think that it helped your opponent. It's unlikely that she would have a 6 in her hand, so unless she flopped a set of 5s, 6s, or 7s or has a pair in the hole, you're still in good shape. Your best guess is that Sandra either has an 8 in her hand or is on a complete bluff.

Because she is a very aggressive player and would be calling the flop and turn with any 8, and because she might suspect that you have a hand like A-K, it makes sense to you that she would try to take the pot away by check-raising with a draw here. At this point there is enough money in the pot for you to have decided to play the hand until the end.

You call her check-raise.

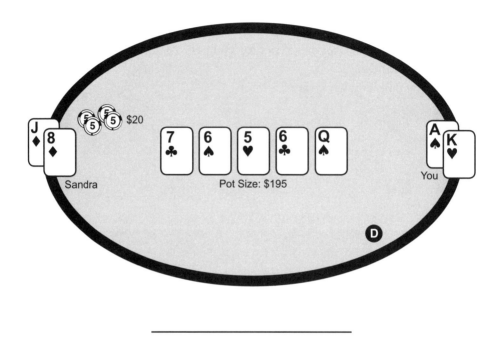

The river brings the Q♠, and Sandra bets again.

You would certainly have preferred to catch an ace or a king, and the queen isn't a great card for you, because among the possible hands you put her on were A-Q and K-Q, but you already made the decision on the turn that you were going to call the river and you're not going to change your mind now.

You call the bet, and win a nice pot.

Notice that the way you decided to play this hand is strongly dependent upon the type of player that you're up against. Had Sandra been a very conservative player, you would've played the hand much differently.

$10-$20 HOLD'EM: NINE-HANDED

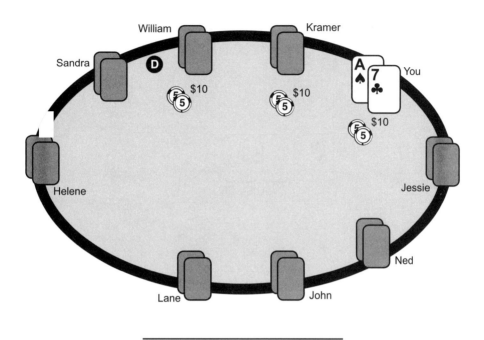

KEY CONCEPTS

- Aggressive play with middle pair
- Isolating an aggressive player
- Putting pressure on a possible draw or mediocre hand

Everybody folds to the button, who flat-calls. The small blind calls as well and you check your A♠ 7♣ in the big blind.

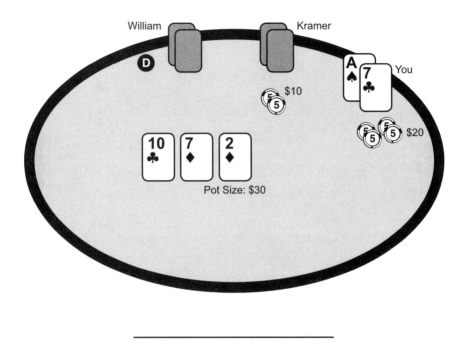

The flop comes 10♣ 7♦ 2♦ and the small blind bets out. You figure the small blind for a hand less than a pair of 10s because you think he would have gone for a check-raise with a pair of 10s or better. You decide that you wanted to try to get heads-up with the small blind, so you raise him, attempting to knock the player on the button out of the hand.

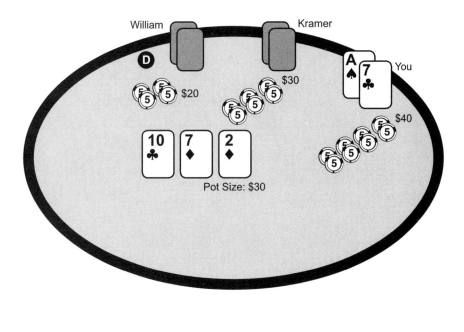

Unfortunately for you, that doesn't work, as the player on the button calls your raise and the small blind reraises. Since you have previously seen the player in the small blind play draws strongly, you think there is a decent chance he is on a draw and that your hand has him beat. You make it four bets, putting extra pressure on the button. Both players call your raise.

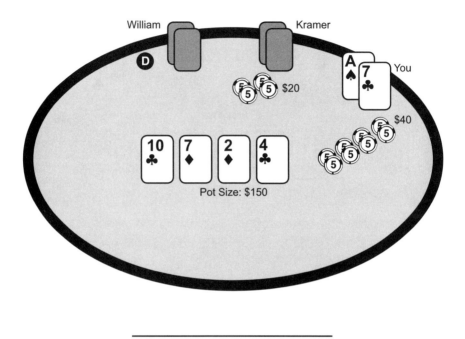

The 4♣ comes on the turn. You don't think that card has helped either player. The small blind bets out again. You still have a strong feeling that you have the small blind beaten, although you aren't sure where the player on the button is. You think there is a good chance that he is on a draw, either diamonds or a hand like 9-8, or that he has top pair. You try to knock him out or make him pay to draw. Therefore, you raise the small blind's bet.

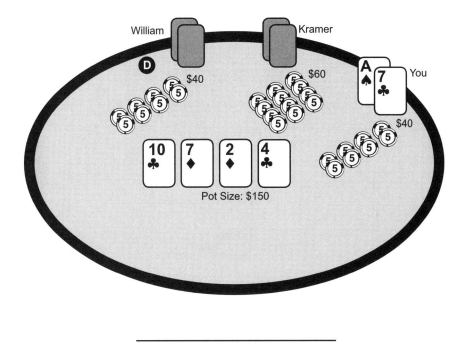

The player on the button calls your raise and the small blind reraises.

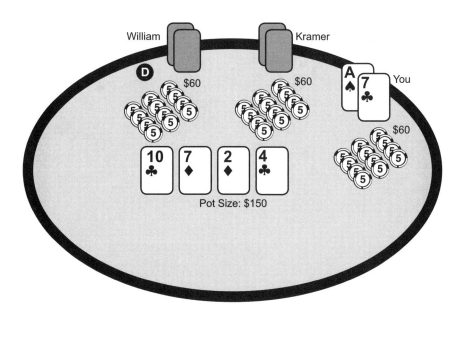

At this point, you think there is a decent chance that you could be beat, but the pot is big enough that you aren't going to fold. You call and the player on the button calls.

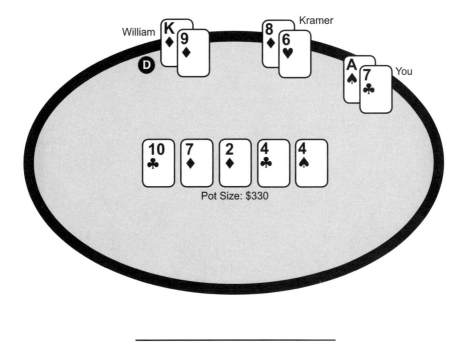

The river pairs the turn card and the small blind checks. Now you have to decide what to do. By this point, if the player on the button has any sort of hand at all, he is going to call you if you bet, and the same goes for the small blind. On the other hand, neither player would call your bet if they both missed their hands. Also, there is a slim chance that the player on the button might bet a missed draw and you could gain an extra bet by calling his bluff.

As it turns out, the player on the button checks his missed draw and you win a huge pot with second pair.

$10-$20 HOLD'EM: TEN-HANDED

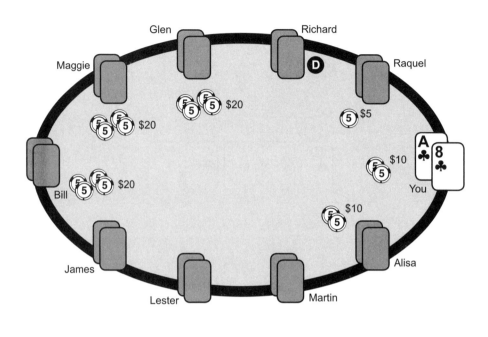

KEY CONCEPTS

• Three-betting to narrow the field and take control of the hand

You have A♣ 8♣ in the big blind. The player under the gun limps. The next three players fold and the player in position No. 7 raises. Positions No. 8 and 9 call. The small blind folds and it's up to you. Some players like to reraise in this spot figuring that at least three of the other players will call and the pot will be a lot bigger if they happen to flop a flush or a flush draw. I don't really like the play for a few reasons. First, the chance of your flopping a flush or a flush draw is remote, and second, in a multiway pot like this you can always make up that extra bet by getting in a check-raise. In addition, the many times that the flop does not help your hand you'll be first to act and won't want to bet. Making it three bets and then checking the flop is not great for your image.

You just call and so does the one remaining player left to act. This is now a five-way pot.

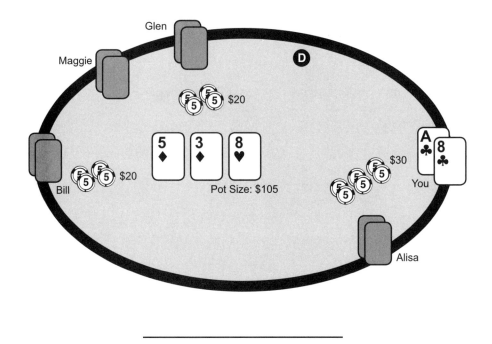

The flop is 5♦ 3♦ 8♥. This is quite a good flop for you and there are two good ways to play it. You can either bet right out, hoping to be raised by the initial raiser or you can go for a check-raise. The advantage of betting right out is that if the early-position player folds and the initial raiser raises, it will put a lot of pressure on the other players and you may be able to get heads-up with only the initial raiser. The disadvantage is that in a five way pot it's quite likely that you will get a lot of callers even if the initial raiser makes it two bets.

You decide to check and see what happens. The early-position player checks and, as you expected, the initial raiser bets. The next player folds and the late-position caller raises. Now you have to assess where you stand and what you want to do. At this point, including you, there are still four players in the pot. You don't put the late-position player on a high pair because you think he would have reraised the initial raiser if he had such a hand. It's possible he flopped a set and is trying to lock out the draws, but you think it's much more likely that he either has an 8 along with you, or is on a draw himself. If there is any way for you to accomplish it, you would like to get heads-up with the late-position player. You know there is a good possibility that the initial raiser doesn't have a pair yet. The best way for you to get heads-up is to make it three bets, and so that's what you do.

The best-possible situation occurs: The early-position player folds, along with the initial raiser. The late-position player calls your raise.

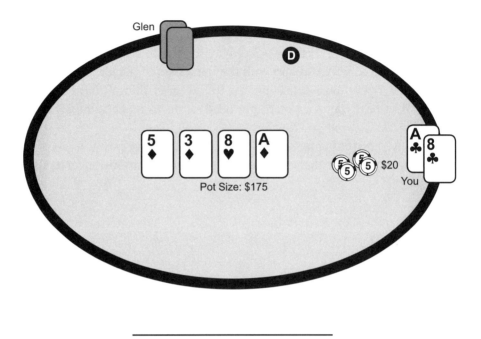

The turn brings the A♦, which is either a very good or very bad card for you. With three diamonds on the board, you can't possibly afford to give a free card. You bet and wait to see what happens. If you get raised, you'll call the raise and check-call on the river unless you fill up. If you are raised and catch an ace on the river, you'll bet out. If you are raised and catch an 8 on the river, you'll go for a check raise. Glen calls your bet.

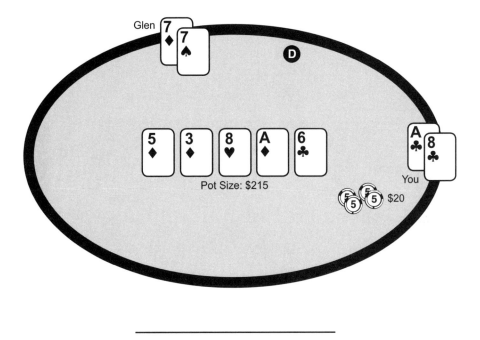

The river brings the 6♣, a relative blank, and you bet one more time. If you get raised here you will certainly call.

Glen calls your bet and you win a nice pot.

$10-$20 HOLD'EM: TEN-HANDED

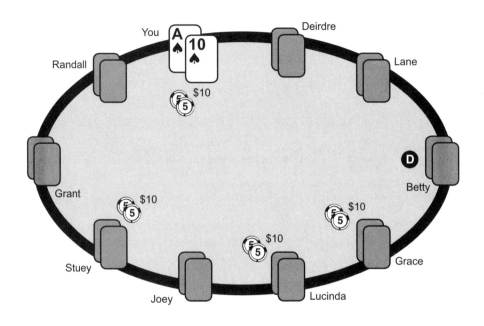

KEY CONCEPTS

- Isolating a bluffer
- Reading the players
- Strong play with a marginal hand

You're in position No. 7 with A♠ 10♠. There's one caller in position No. 4 before it gets to you. You don't usually raise with this hand in a full ring game unless you're close to or on the button. This is the type of hand that plays better multiway. Also, by raising in middle position with this hand you are likely to knock out the types of hands you want to be playing against, specifically aces or 10s with a worse kicker. This means hands like A-8, A-4, K-10, J-10, and similar hands.

The players in the last three positions fold, the small blind calls, and the big blind checks. It's now a four-way pot and you'll be last to act throughout the hand.

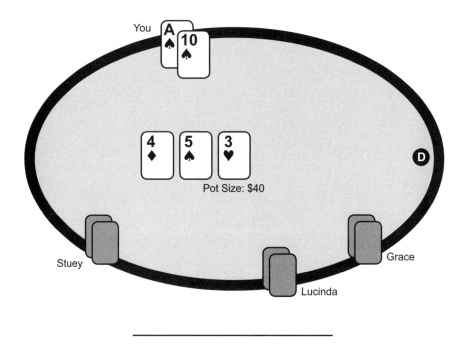

The flop comes 4♦ 5♠ 3♥ and everyone checks to you. Although there's a decent chance that you have the best hand, there is also a good chance with a board like this that if you bet you will be check-raised by one of the blinds. You'd rather take a free card, so you check as well.

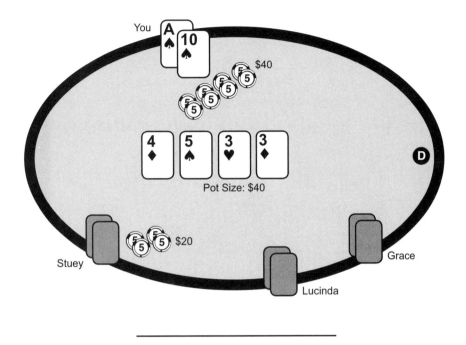

The turn pairs the board and both blinds check. Stuey bets. The easy play is to fold, but many times the easy play is not the best way to make the most money. You're not sure what the players in the blinds have, but you're pretty sure that at best they have a draw. Were they to have any piece of the board, they probably would have bet the turn to avoid giving another free card since everybody checked on the flop.

The bet from Stuey smells pretty fishy. Either he flopped a monster or he has no pair. You think it's a lot more likely that he has a hand like K-J or Q-J than that he has any piece of the board. If he had a high pair, A-K, A-Q, or probably even A-J, he would have raised it coming in. If he had a medium pair he would have bet the flop to avoid giving three players a free card to beat him.

You decide that there is a very good chance that you have Stuey beat, but calling is a terrible option. Your best play is to raise him and try to take the pot right here. At the very least, you'd like to knock out the two blinds and get heads-up with him.

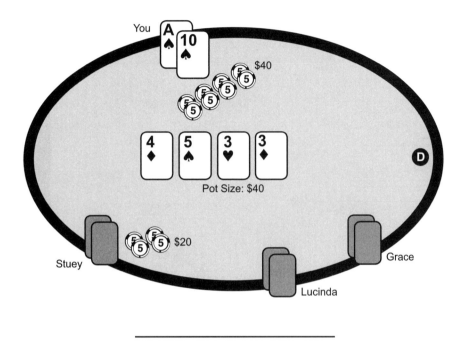

As it turns out, you read him correctly; your raise knocks out the other players, and he folds as well.

$10-$20 HOLD'EM: NINE-HANDED

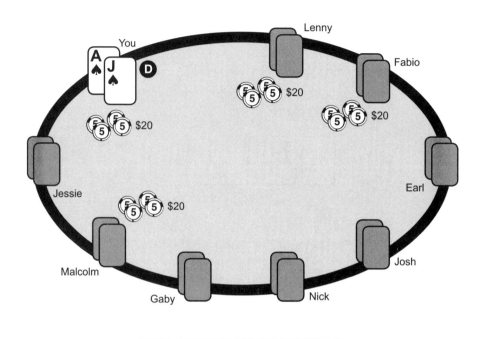

![KEY CONCEPTS]

KEY CONCEPTS

- Folding top pair
- Mixing up your play

You have A♠ J♠ suited on the button. Everybody has folded to the player in position No. 7, who raises. Although you think there is a very good chance that you have the best hand, you have a suited ace, which plays well multiway. You like to mix up your play a bit so you just call. Both the small and big blinds call as well. Time to see the flop.

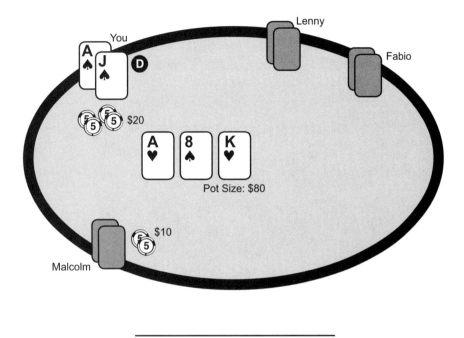

The flop comes A♥ 8♠ K♥ and both blinds check. The initial raiser bets. Since you have an ace with a good kicker, the raise before the flop came from late position, and you don't want to let anybody draw at either a flush or a straight cheaply, you raise.

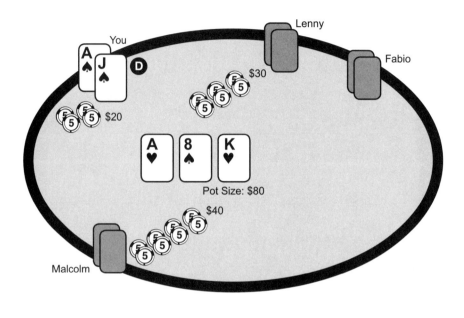

The small blind makes it three bets and the initial raiser caps it. Since you can't think of two hands these players are likely to have that you can beat, and the odds of drawing out if you don't have the best hand seem slim, it's an easy fold for you.

$10-$20 HOLD'EM: NINE-HANDED

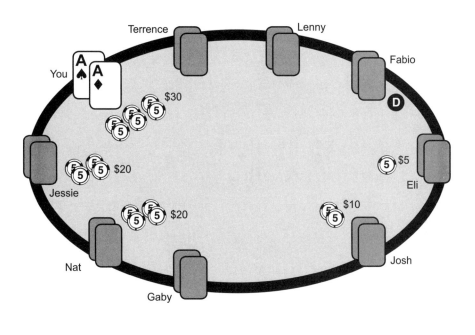

KEY CONCEPTS

- Playing an overpair strongly
- Isolating a weak hand

In this example, you play your pocket aces strongly to avoid giving any cheap or free cards to other players. One player has raised and another has called in front of you. You make it three bets to get more money in the pot and to narrow down the field. The players behind you as well as the two blinds fold. Both the initial raiser and the player who called his raise call.

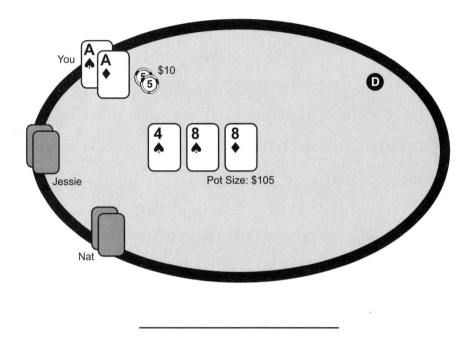

The flop comes 4♠ 8♠ 8♦ and both players check to you. There's no reason to be afraid that one of the other players has an 8, and a check would look too suspicious, so you bet. Both players call.

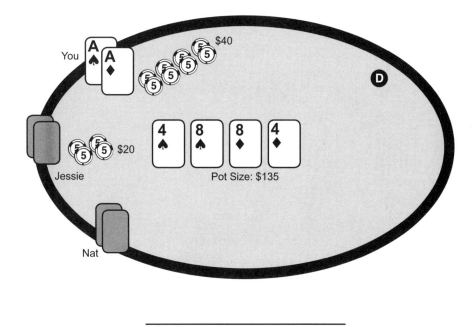

The 4♦ on the turn puts a second pair on the board as well as a second flush draw. The initial raiser checks and Jessie bets. It certainly doesn't make any sense that he would have either an 8 or a 4 in his hand.

You raise for two reasons. First, because you think you have the best hand so you'd like to get more money in the pot. Second, to knock out the other player. Nat folds and Jessie calls your raise.

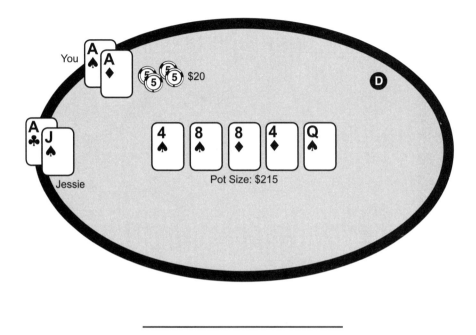

The Q♠ on the river completes the flush draw and Jesse checks to you. Even though the flush draw got there, you don't hesitate to bet your hand for value.

Jesse calls your river bet and you win a nice-sized pot.

$10-$20 HOLD'EM: TEN-HANDED

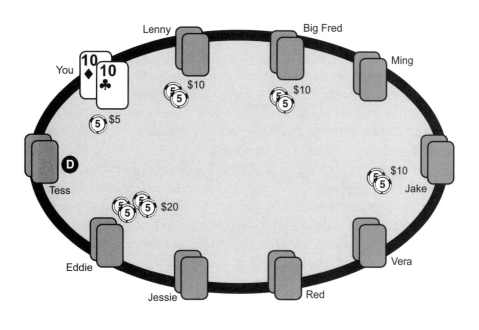

 KEY CONCEPTS

- Playing a medium pair from the small blind
- Check-raising to isolate
- Betting for value and protection
- Calling a raise on the turn after you check-raised the flop

Here's a situation in which you have a strong hand that doesn't do well against multiple players unless it improves. There is a caller under the gun and another caller in position No. 5. The cutoff raises. A raise by the cutoff in this situation indicates a strong hand because he is raising two early-position callers, so he knows he will be getting action. He also knows it is likely he will have to show down a hand to win the pot because he will probably pick up at least one of the blinds. That means a four-way pot, which usually ends with hands being shown down.

You have pocket 10s on the small blind and just call, taking a wait-and-see attitude. If you thought you could get it heads-up or even three way, you'd reraise, but there is very little chance of that here. Reraising has another disadvantage in that you would be building such a large pot that most of the players will be forced to take a card off on the turn. Even if you check-raise on the flop, many players will take a card off with just overcards if you three-bet preflop and make a large enough pot.

By playing this way, if you get a flop of small cards you can go for a check-raise and have a decent chance to narrow the field. This is true for two reasons. First, the pot will be smaller than if you try to make it three bets, so players will be less likely to feel calling two bets cold is worth it, and, second, small cards are less likely to fit into their hands. If the flop comes two high cards, you can get away from your hand with a minimum investment. The big blind calls, and it is now a five-way pot.

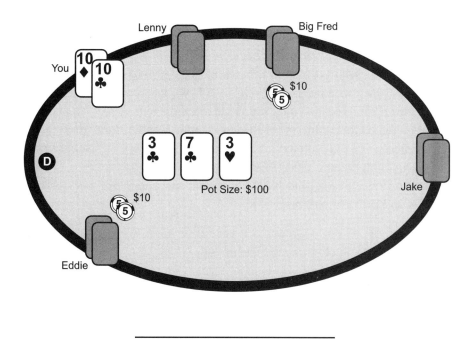

The flop comes 3♣ 7♣ 3♥, a great result for you. This is definitely time to go for a check-raise. You'd like to get heads-up with the raiser if possible. Unless he has a pair of jacks, queens, kings, aces, a set of 7s, A-3, or a pair of 3s, you have him in bad shape. (There is little reason to worry about 7-3.) You check, the big blind checks, and the under-the-gun caller bets. The player in position No. 5 folds and the initial raiser just calls. This is a strong indication that you have the best hand.

Why? The player under the gun most likely has a pair like 9s or 8s or A-7 suited. It is unlikely he has a pair of jacks or higher because he would have raised coming in. It is possible that he has a hand like A-3 suited, but it is still safe to assume that you have him beat so far.

The initial raiser probably doesn't have a pair of 10s beat

because he would usually raise the bettor if he did. With jacks, queens, or kings, he'd raise because he would not want an ace to fall and kill his hand. Even if he had a pair of aces, he probably would raise to avoid letting someone develop a draw on the turn.

Now is a good time to check-raise for value and take control of the hand. Many times in this situation, you will be up against a smaller pair (which has two outs), and two overcards, (which has six outs). This means you are up against eight outs twice. An added advantage is that someone with two overcards might think there is a decent chance that you have a 3 and fold to your check-raise, giving you an even better chance to win the pot.

You check-raise, the big blind folds, the under-the-gun player calls and the original raiser folds.

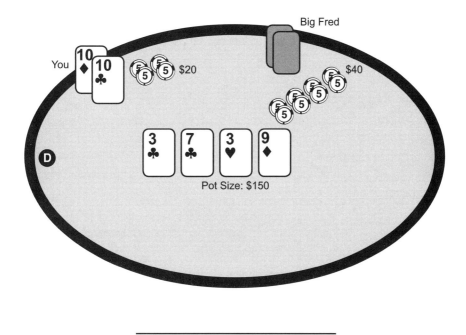

The turn brings the 9♦. You should almost always bet out in this spot unless you have an excellent tell on your one remaining opponent.

Big Fred raises you. Now it is time to decide what he is likely to have. He is representing a 3, pocket 7s, or pocket 9s. But are these hands likely? The most likely is pocket 9s. If he has that, you will just have to pay him off. The second most likely hand is A-3 suited. You will also have to pay him off if he has that. Big Fred could also be raising with A-7, A♣ 9♣, 8♣ 9♣, 9♣ 10♣, 8-8, or hands like 5♣ 6♣, 6♣ 8♣, 7-9 suited, or even a pair of 6s or 5s.

You call the raise. At this point you're pretty committed to the pot. In the long run, you'll lose too much by folding here unless you really know the player and you're certain that he would not be playing the hand this way with anything less than a pair of jacks.

You could also reraise and then call all the way if you are raised again. This would be a reasonable way to play the hand against aggressive opponents.

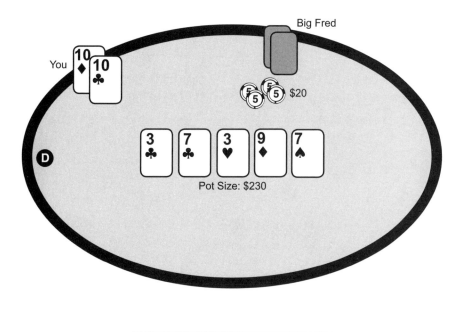

The river brings the 7♠. This is not a great card for you, but not that bad either. Any draws have missed. Any hand with two overcards has missed as well. The only likely hands that beat you are A-3, A-7, pocket 3s, pocket 7s, and pocket 9s.

You check. Your opponent bets.

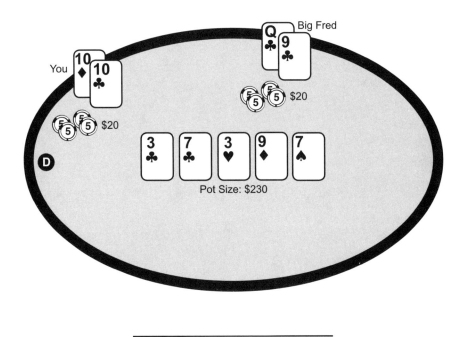

You call and take down the pot.

$10-$20 HOLD'EM: NINE-HANDED

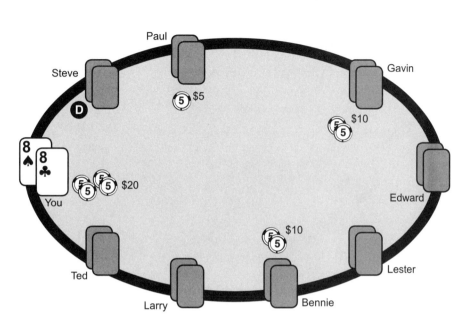

KEY CONCEPTS

- Playing a middle pair
- Protecting your hand
- Not giving free cards
- Continuation bets

You have a medium pair (8♠ 8♣) in late position. One player has limped in, which is not an indication of strength. Chances are that you have the best hand so far. You raise to try to knock out the blinds and play heads-up against the limper. If the blinds fold, they'll be leaving some dead money in the pot and make it more likely your 8s will hold up as the best hand. If they call, you don't mind playing it multiway with a lot of money in the pot in case you are lucky enough to flop a set.

The button folds, the small blind calls, the big blind folds, and the limper calls. Time to see the flop.

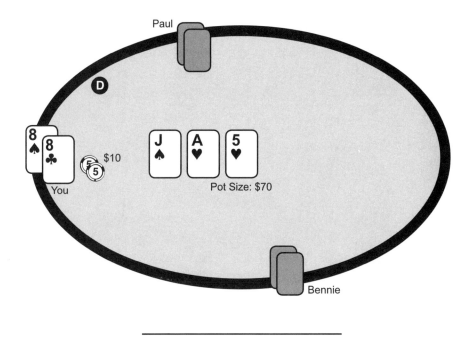

The flop is J♠ A♥ 5♥, not the flop you were hoping for, but both players check to you. Since you raised before the flop, there is a very good chance that you could have a piece of this flop. In this situation, you almost always bet to see if you can win the pot uncontested. If you get called, you'll try to check it down unless you hit an 8. If you get check-raised, it's an easy fold.

You bet and both of your opponents fold.

$10-$20 HOLD'EM: NINE-HANDED

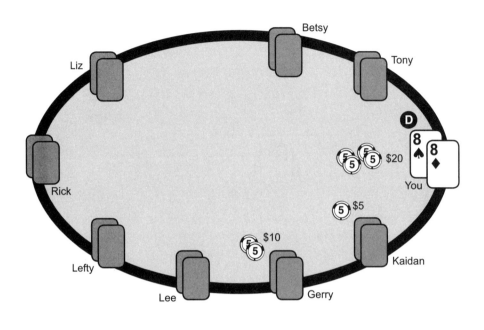

KEY CONCEPTS

• Getting check-raised from the blinds
• Playing middle pairs
• Not giving free cards

Here's another hand in which you have a medium pair (8♠ 8♦) in late position, this time on the button. Everyone has folded to you, so of course you raise. You'd be happy to pick up the blinds here, but if you get one or two callers, you'll probably be playing the best hand.

Both blinds call.

The fact that you did not get raised makes you even more sure that you have the best hand so far.

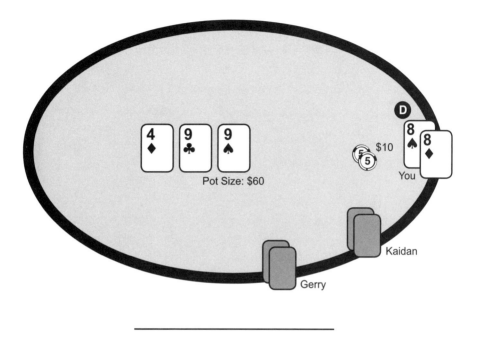

The flop, 4♦ 9♣ 9♠, is excellent for you. Unless someone has a 9, pocket fours, or slowplayed a big pair, you have way the best of it. Both players check to you and of course you bet again. This would be a very bad time to give a free card. In a situation like this, you have to bet to protect your hand because it is too vulnerable to any high cards that might fall.

Although the small blind folds, the big blind check-raises you. You often expect that in this kind of situation. After all, you raised on the button when everyone folded to you. There is a very good chance that you don't have much of a hand, and if you do it's likely to be two high cards. Many blind-position players try to put pressure on late-position raisers when low cards flop.

You still think the chance is excellent that you have the best hand. You could call and then pop it on the turn, but you decide to play it fast here. Rather than give the player a free card, you reraise.

Sure enough, your assessment of the situation was correct and your opponent decides he doesn't have enough of a hand to continue. Chances are his reraise was a total bluff. He folds.

$10-$20 HOLD'EM: NINE-HANDED

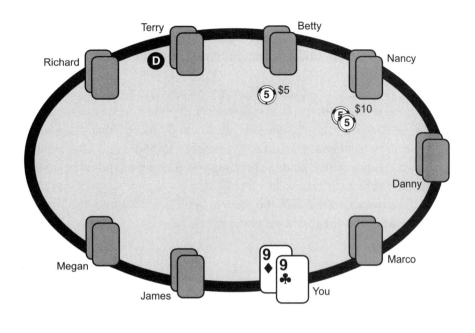

![KEY CONCEPTS]

KEY CONCEPTS

- Reading players
- Playing middle pairs
- Determining the texture of the flop

You have a pair of 9s in position No. 5. The first two players fold and it's up to you. There are two ways to play a medium pair under these circumstances. You can either raise and try to take control of the pot, or you can simply call and see what the other players decide to do. The advantage of raising is that you may be able to narrow the field and give your medium pair a better chance to win without improving. Playing it that way presents some problems because you often will be called by players with better position than you and often overcards will flop. If so, you won't know where you stand and usually will have to bet into a scary board. Players behind you will then often call whether they have you beaten or not, so you will also be faced with difficult decisions on the turn. If the flop brings even one overcard and you bet out and get raised, you will have a difficult choice.

If, instead, you flat-call before the flop, you can get away from the hand with minimum loss if you don't like the flop, and you often can get a check-raise or three bets in if you do like it. Your decision about how to play a hand like this before the flop should be based on who your opponents are, the tempo of the game, and what your current table image is.

You decide to flat-call, the players behind you all fold, the small blind calls, and the big blind checks.

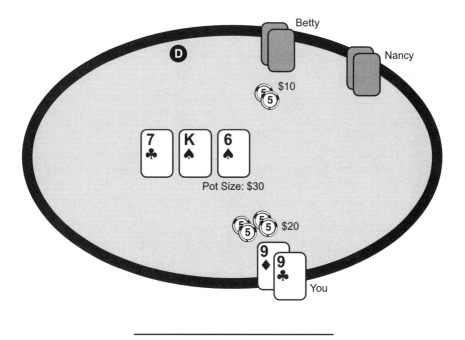

The flop brings 7♣ K♠ 6♠ and the small blind bets out. The big blind folds and it's up to you. You are not convinced that the small blind has you beaten at this point. There are both flush and straight draws out there, as well as two smallish cards. You think there is a good likelihood that Betty has either a 6, a 7, or a draw. If she has a king, the chances are good that she has a weak kicker.

You raise to see what she does.

Betty reraises, which makes you think it is a bit more likely that she is on a draw. Many players overplay draws heads-up in an attempt to make the other player fold. There is also the possibility that she has a strong hand and wants to make sure you don't get a free card, but your gut feel is that she is on a draw. Given the flop, the chance that Betty has a king with a good kicker or two pair is not nearly as likely as the chance that she is on a draw. If she had a king with a mediocre or bad kicker, she would not reraise here, because she would be afraid she was beaten. After all, you limped in from middle position, making it quite likely that you have a hand like K-Q, K-J, or K-10 suited.

You call Betty's raise, with the intention of calling her down to the end unless the board becomes too scary.

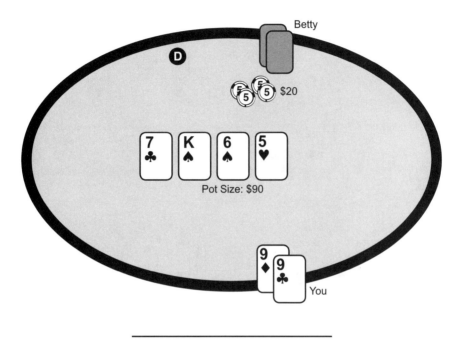

The turn brings the 5♥ and Betty bets out. This is not a particularly good card for you because it makes her a straight if she is holding 8-9. On the other hand, if she was on a draw other than 7♠ 5♠ and did not make a straight, you still have the best hand.

You call.

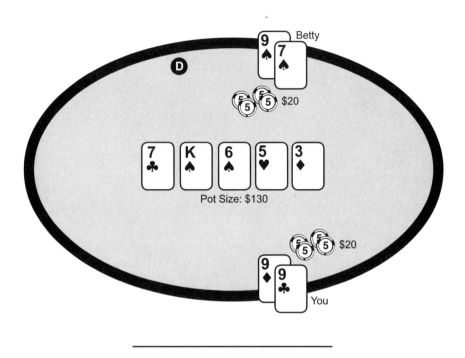

The river brings the 3♦. If Betty has 8-9 or a 4, she has a straight. If she was on a spade draw, you almost surely have the best hand. Betty bets the river and you are getting 7.5 to 1 to call. You think there is a much better than 7.5 to 1 chance that you have the best hand, so you call. And, in this case, you win.

$10-$20 HOLD'EM: TEN-HANDED

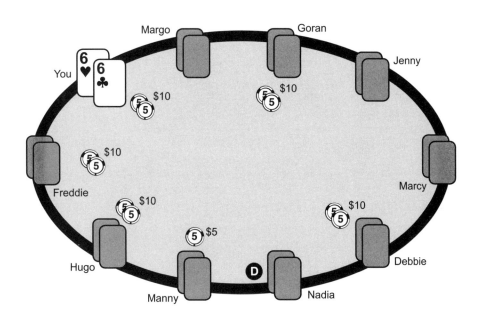

KEY CONCEPTS

- Dealing with scare cards
- Playing middle pairs
- Implied odds
- Reading players
- Protecting your hand

Normally I'm not crazy about playing a small pair in early position in a full game, but here's a good time to do it. There's already one caller before you, so you think there is a good chance that this pot may develop into a five- or six-way hand. You have pocket 6s. You'd like to try to flop a set against a lot of opponents, so you call.

Two other players come in behind you, the small blind calls, and the big blind raises. You don't mind this as now five other players are contesting the pot and the odds against flopping a set are about 7.5 to 1. If you do hit a set, you will probably win the hand, making your implied odds much greater than the current 5 to 1 you are getting on your money.

You call. The other players call as well, making it a six-way pot.

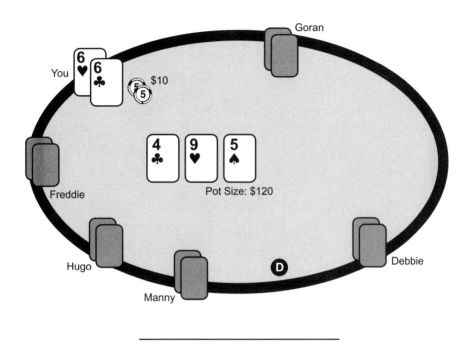

The flop comes 4♣ 9♥ 5♠. The small blind checks, as do the big blind raiser and Freddie in position No. 3. Now it's up to you. Although there is a chance that the big blind is slowplaying a high pair or a set, you think it is a lot more likely that he has a suited hand like K-Q or J-10. Many players like to raise with that type of hand from the blinds in multiway pots.

You decide that, unless someone has a 9, there is a good chance you have the best hand so far. You'd like to try to protect it, so you bet out, knowing there is a good chance you may be raised. You actually don't mind being raised by one of the two players behind you, because people in those positions with two overcards often will raise an early-position bettor in this situation to increase their chances of winning if they catch a pair.

Goran folds, Debbie calls, the small blind folds, and both Hugo and Freddie call. That makes you even more sure that you have the best hand at this point. That Hugo, the big blind, didn't check-raise all but rules out the possibility that he has a set or a high pocket pair.

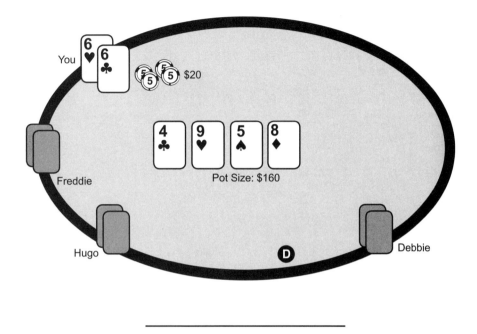

The turn brings an offsuit 8 and Hugo and Freddie check to you. You bet your hand both for value and to put pressure on your opponents to fold. Debbie folds, as does Hugo, but Freddie calls.

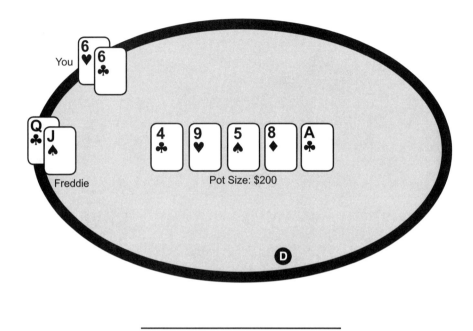

An ace comes on the river and Freddie checks to you. You're pretty sure he doesn't have a 9 or a straight, but you think he could have a pair of 7s, a hand like 8-7, or perhaps an ace. It's not unlikely that he has something like A-Q, A-J, or A-10, A-5, or A-4. After the ace falls, there is little reason to bet your 6s for value, because the only hands that are likely to call you are ones that have you beat. You check.

You dodge a bullet and you win a nice pot with a small pair that never improved.

$10-$20 HOLD'EM: EIGHT-HANDED

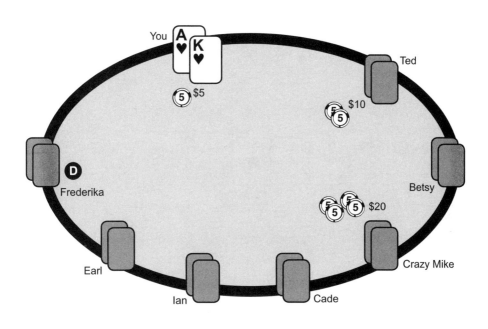

- Waiting until the flop to put in extra bets
- Small blind play
- Isolating a probable worse hand
- Betting overcards for value
- Not giving free cards

You have A♥ K♥ in the small blind. The player in position No. 4 raises, and everybody else folds around to you. There are a few different ways to play this hand. There's a good chance that you have the best hand, so reraising would not be a bad play, but it would give away the strength of your hand. You normally prefer to play A-K heads-up, but since you are suited and can almost surely get a check-raise you don't mind letting the big blind in.

You just call, as does the big blind.

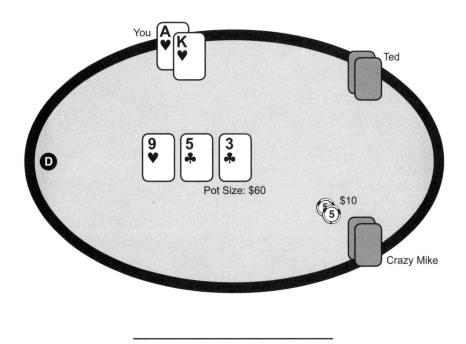

The flop comes 9♥ 5♣ 3♣. Although you think there is a very good chance you have the best hand, you check to see what happens. The big blind also checks and the initial raiser bets.

This is where you take control of the pot. As mentioned, you think there is an excellent chance that you have the best hand, so you check-raise, hoping to knock the big blind out and get heads-up with the initial raiser.

The big blind folds and the initial raiser calls your check-raise.

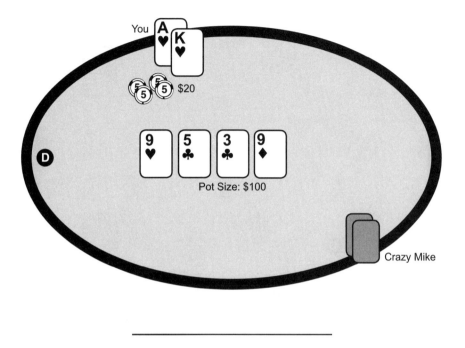

The turn brings the 9♦, which pairs the highest card on the board, and is a good result for you. You're pretty sure that Crazy Mike does not have a 9, but the way you played the hand makes it seem likely that you might. You can be sure that if you had the best hand on the flop, you still do.

You bet out and take the pot.

$15-$30 HOLD'EM: TEN-HANDED

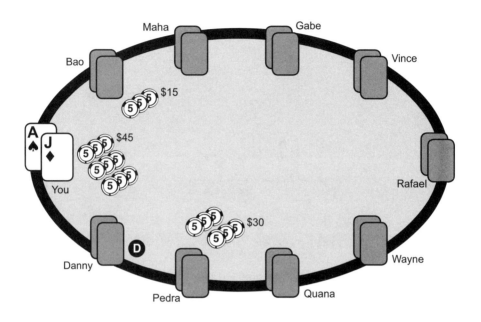

KEY CONCEPTS

- Don't get bluffed out
- Three-betting from the small blind
- Taking control of a hand
- Semibluffing
- Reading an aggressive opponent

Here's a situation that you will find yourself in often. Everybody has folded to the cutoff, who has raised, the button has folded, and you have a good ace (A♠ J♦) in the small blind.

In this situation, I suggest a reraise about 75 percent of the time. If you're suited, which means your hand plays well multiway, you can sometimes just call and allow the big blind to come in. On this hand, you decide to reraise, hoping to knock out the big blind and get some dead money in the pot. When you're pretty sure you have the best hand, you should often try to take the lead. In a spot like this, if you get heads-up with the cutoff, you're often willing to play to the end even if you don't improve.

The big blind folds and the cutoff calls your reraise.

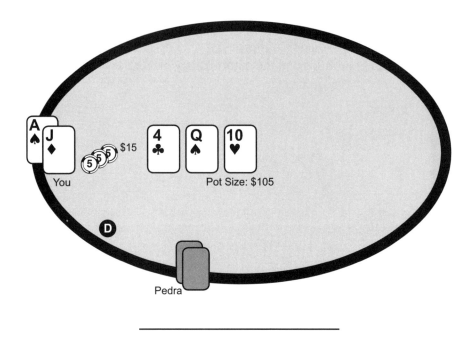

The flop comes 4♣ Q♠ 10♥, which gives you a gutshot straight draw and an overcard. Even though this is a rather dangerous board for you, you bet out.

Your opponent calls.

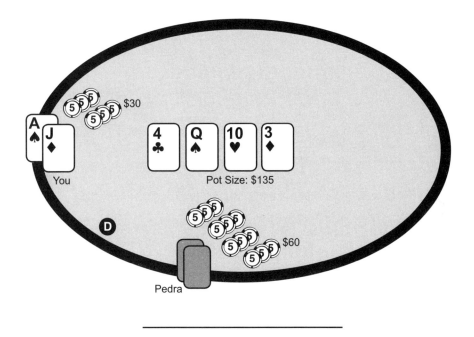

The turn brings a blank, the 3♦, and since you have not received any indication that you do not have the best hand, you bet out again.

This time Pedra raises you and you have to decide what type of hand she is likely to have. She could have a hand like A-Q, A-10, or even Q-10. Interestingly enough, whether she has one pair with A-Q or two pair with Q-10 makes no difference to you, as you have four outs in both situations. If she has A-10, you have seven outs: four kings and three jacks.

You know that Pedra is a pretty aggressive player who likes to try to steal pots heads-up when she thinks she has a chance to do so. Therefore, you think there is a decent chance that she could be raising you with any draw or even a hand like 9-10. There is also the possibility that she's on a complete bluff.

If she's on a draw, you have the best hand. If Pedra has a pair of queens with a kicker other than an ace, you have seven outs. If she has a hand like 10-9 you have ten outs. The pot is offering you 7.5 to 1, so it is an easy call.

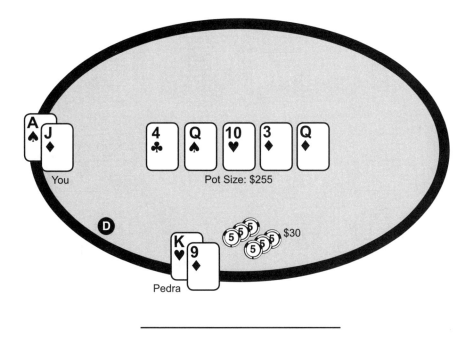

The river pairs the queen and you check to her. This is actually not a bad card for you because, although you did not complete your hand, you are still ahead if she had any draw.

Pedra bets the river.

Including her river bet, there are 9.5 big bets in the pot. You figure with this particular player there is at least a 1 in 10 chance that she has a busted hand, so you call.

You win a nice pot with ace high.

Bear in mind that you have to know the player to play the hand as you did here.

$10-$20 HOLD'EM: NINE-HANDED

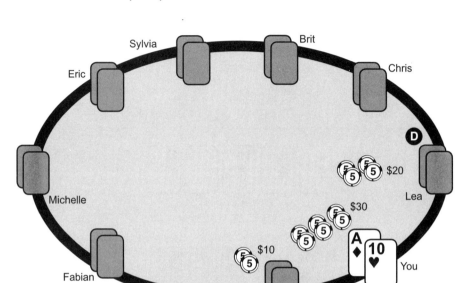

![KEY CONCEPTS]

- Taking control of a hand
- Aggressive play for value
- Three-betting from the small blind

You are in the small blind and everybody has folded to a fairly aggressive player who is on the button and raises. You have a pretty good ace (A♦ 10♥). Your hand being unsuited plays better heads-up. You therefore reraise to try to knock out the big blind and in the process get some dead money in the pot.

The big blind folds, and the player on the button reraises you. You call.

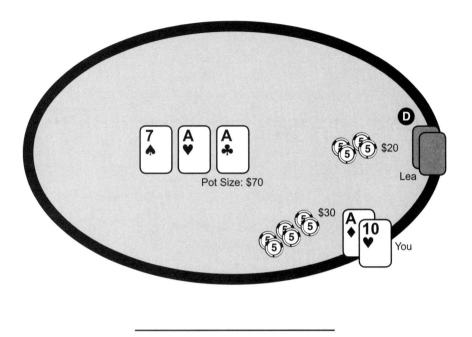

The flop comes 7♠ A♥ A♣, and you bet right out with your three aces. Sometimes that is a better play than trying for a check-raise. If you check in this spot, a player without an ace will often check behind you. When you bet out, many opponents do not believe you have an ace and give you more action than if you try for a check-raise. As you expected, the player on the button raises you, and you make it three bets.

The button calls.

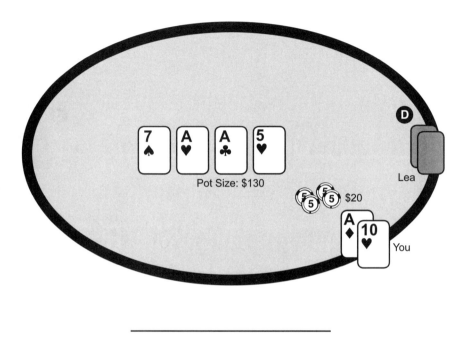

The turn brings the 5♥, a blank. You've made the decision to play your three aces for the best hand all the way through. You bet, hoping not to get raised, but planning to call to the end even if you do.

Your opponent flat-calls. Had Lea raised you here, you would probably just call and check-call on the end unless you hit your kicker, in which case you would go for a check-raise. If she raised you here on the turn and the board paired on the end you would bet out. That's because you'd be afraid that she would check a pocket pair on the end but you would not lose to any ace with a higher kicker than yours.

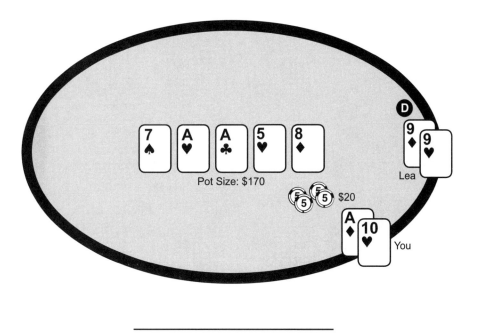

The river produces the 8♦ and you make one last value bet, knowing that the pot is so large that Lea is likely to call with any pair, but probably wouldn't bet anything less than three aces.

Lea calls. As it turns out, she had a pocket pair and you make maximum value on the hand.

$15-$30 HOLD'EM: TEN-HANDED

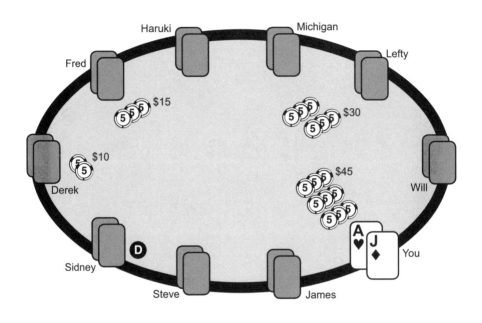

- Three-betting to narrow the field
- Continuation bets
- Betting for value

You have A♥ J♦ in position No. 7. The first two players fold and the player in position No. 5 raises. In this situation, I recommend either folding or raising. Merely calling is generally bad, because then it is likely that a few other players will come in and you will be playing a hand that plays well only against one or two players in a pot with four or five. If you reraise with this hand, you often can get the other players to fold, thereby getting some dead money in the pot, which increases your pot odds. Also, you gain control of the hand. If you get reraised, you know you have to hit the flop well to continue.

You reraise, and all the other players fold to the initial raiser, who calls your bet.

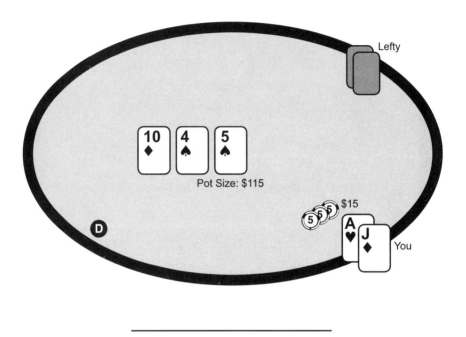

The flop comes 10♦ 4♠ 5♠, and the initial raiser checks to you. Although you have nothing, there is a decent chance that you have the best hand, and you reraised before the flop, so you bet. You don't want to give any free cards here to hands like A-9, K-Q, or K-J. You also want to give a hand like A-Q a chance to fold. If you get check-raised, you will take into account what type of player you are up against and likely fold on the turn if you don't hit an ace or a jack.

Lefty calls your bet.

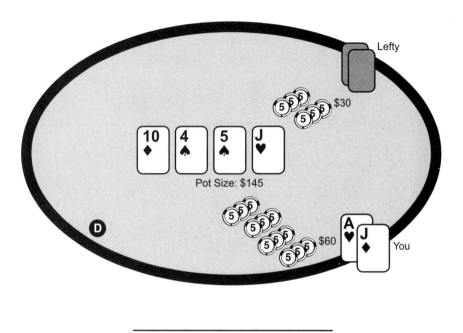

The turn brings a jack, and your opponent bets out. This a great card for you and you are almost certain that you have the best hand, so you raise. The only hand that makes any sense for Lefty to have that would have you beat is J-10. That's not likely, because he probably wouldn't raise in position No. 5 before the flop with that hand, and if he did have that hand he probably would have bet or check-raised on the flop. You don't think he has a set or an overpair, because he would have reraised you on the flop, or capped it before the flop.

You raise and Lefty calls your raise.

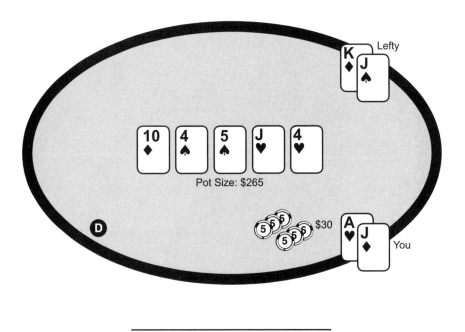

The river pairs the 4. Regardless of what card came on the river, you would bet for value. You would not hesitate to bet even if a king, queen, or spade came. If your opponent bet into you on the river, you would just call.

You bet and Lefty calls.

You were able to get maximum value on every round due to aggressive play regardless of whether your hand was, at the time, marginal or strong.

SECTION

11

FINAL THOUGHTS

Poker is like life. There are few hard and fast rules. You learn by doing. This book has provided many examples of how various hands could be profitably played and how you must adjust your strategy to the player, the situation, and the dynamics of the table. Plays that work against one player might not work against another. Plays you make against a particular opponent might work for you once, but fail later in the evening or on another occasion when the mood is different or circumstances have changed.

As an aspiring expert limit hold'em player, one of the most important concepts that we hope you have learned is that there is no one correct way to play the majority of the hands that you'll be dealt. Your goal should be to have a thorough understanding of the concepts we've discussed in this book and be able to incorporate them into your play. Further, you should be willing to play the same hand various ways on different occasions against the same opponents so that they will not be able to accurately read your actions. It's crucial to keep your opponents guessing to make it difficult for them to play you properly.

Although it's important to get the basics of solid play under your belt, if you want to win the big money you will have to think deeply about what makes your opponents tick. In fact, the higher the limits you play, the clearer it will become that poker is more a game of *people* than it is a game of cards.

To be a winner, you must adhere to a conservative bankroll management strategy and bring your "A" game to the table. *Always*. And you must also have a thorough understanding of your own psychological makeup and emotional state during sessions. If you are playing in such a way that your edge has disappeared, it is usually time to quit.

Remember that the sum total of all of the sessions you play equals one long game and the best way for you to insure that you come out a winner is to be up to the challenge. We've given you many of the tools you'll need to beat your tougher opponents. Use these tools wisely and you'll be well on your way to becoming a top player.

The Dumbest Kid in the World

A young boy enters a barber shop and the barber whispers to his customer, "This is the dumbest kid in the world. Watch while I prove it to you."

The barber puts a dollar bill in one hand and two quarters in the other, then calls the boy over and asks, "Which do you want, son?" The boy takes the quarters and leaves.

"What did I tell you?" said the barber. "That kid never learns!"

Later, when the customer leaves, he sees the same young boy coming out of the ice cream store. "Hey, son! May I ask you a question? Why did you take the quarters instead of the dollar bill?"

The boy licks his cone and replies, "Because the day I take the dollar, the game's over!"

Appendix A

OUTS, ODDS, AND PERCENTAGES

THE CONCEPT OF OUTS

When we refer to outs, we mean the cards that will result in your hand being the best hand in a showdown. For instance, if you have a heart flush draw on the turn and you know for certain that making the flush will win you the pot, your outs would be the nine remaining hearts. If you were holding A-K on the turn and had no pair and your opponent had one pair with a kicker other than an ace or a king, so that you knew for certain that pairing either your ace or your king would win the pot, then your outs would be the three remaining aces and the three remaining kings. In that situation you would have six outs.

Examining the first situation a bit further, suppose you had a heart flush draw on the turn, but another player in the hand had a higher heart flush draw. If you are heads-up with that player and neither one of you has yet made a pair, and neither one of you has a straight draw along with the flush draw, then you have six outs. Those six outs would not be the hearts, but they would be the six remaining cards in the deck that would give you a pair. For example, suppose you have 8♥ 7♥, your opponent has A♥ K♥, and the board reads 2♥ 6♥ Q♦ 2♣. A heart on the end would do you no good because, although you would make a flush, your opponent would make a higher flush. The only cards that would do you any good would be the three remaining 7s and the three remaining 8s. Therefore, you would have six outs in that situation.

Examining this situation a bit further, suppose you hold A♥ K♥

and your opponent holds 8♣ 6♣. You are heads-up on the turn and the board reads 2♦ 7♣ 8♥ 3♠. Only an ace or a king will make yours the best hand, and neither card will improve your opponent's hand. If you do not catch an ace or a king, your opponent will beat you with at least a pair of 8s. Therefore, you have six outs: the three remaining aces and the three remaining kings.

One of the problems with trying to determine the number of outs you have is that you can never really be certain what your opponents have. Sometimes you can be sure that a certain number of cards are definitely outs for you while other cards may be outs for you.

An example of this is when you have A♠ 10♠ and the board reads Q♠ 7♠ 4♥ 2♣. You know that any spade that does not pair the board is an out for you. It is also possible that a spade that does pair the board is an out for you and that an ace and possibly even a 10 are also outs. If you knew that all of those cards were really outs, then you would have nine spades, three aces, and three 10s, for a total of 15 outs. In situations like this you might want to assume that you have 8.5 outs for the spades and perhaps another 2.5 outs for the times that an ace or 10 wins you the pot, for a total of 11 outs.

When figuring your outs on the flop, you also have to consider the cards that might allow your opponent to redraw on you. For instance, if you are drawing to a straight and there are two diamonds on the board, your true outs are less than eight cards twice because someone may make a flush if a diamond falls on the river. This is not an exact science, because you are missing so much information. You just have to make your best estimate of what your opponents have in order to decide what your likely number of outs is.

ODDS AND PERCENTAGES FOR THE FLOP AND TURN

The following tables present the odds and percentages for various numbers of outs on the flop and on the turn. On the flop, you have two cards to come and on the turn you have one card to come. If you miss your hand after drawing on the flop, the odds against making the hand on the turn are approximately twice what they would be on the flop. The corresponding percentage (chance) of making the hand is approximately half on the turn of what it is on the flop.

Precise Figures

These two tables show the odds and percentages to one decimal place.

TWO CARDS TO COME

OUTS	ODDS	PERCENTAGE
1	22.5 to 1	4.3%
2	10.88 to 1	8.4%
3	7.01 to 1	12.5%
4	5.07 to 1	16.5%
5	3.91 to 1	20.4%
6	3.14 to 1	24.1%
7	2.59 to 1	27.8%
8	2.18 to 1	31.5%
9	1.86 to 1	35.0%
10	1.60 to 1	38.4%
11	1.40 to 1	41.7%
12	1.22 to 1	45.0%
13	1.08 to 1	48.1%
14	1 to 1.05	51.2%
15	1 to 1.18	54.1%
16	1 to 1.32	57.0%
17	1 to 1.49	59.8%
18	1 to 1.66	62.4%
19	1 to 1.86	65.0%
20	1 to 2.08	67.5%

ONE CARD TO COME

OUTS	ODDS	PERCENTAGE
1	45 to 1	2.2%
2	22 to 1	4.3%
3	14.33 to 1	6.5%
4	10.50 to 1	8.7%
5	8.20 to 1	10.9%
6	6.67 to 1	13.0%
7	5.57 to 1	15.2%
8	4.75 to 1	17.4%
9	4.11 to 1	19.6%
10	3.60 to 1	21.7%
11	3.18 to 1	23.9%
12	2.83 to 1	26.1%
13	2.54 to 1	28.3%
14	2.29 to 1	30.4%
15	2.07 to 1	32.6%
16	1.88 to 1	34.8%
17	1.71 to 1	37.0%
18	1.56 to 1	39.1%
19	1.42 to 1	41.3%
20	1.30 to 1	43.5%

Approximate Figures

Here are the same tables with the odds and percentages rounded off. You will probably find it a lot easier to use these versions. It would be a good idea for you to commit these numbers to memory.

TWO CARDS TO COME

OUTS	ODDS	PERCENTAGE
1	22.5 to 1	4.0%
2	11 to 1	8.0%
3	7 to 1	13.0%
4	5 to 1	17.0%
5	4 to 1	20.0%
6	3.25 to 1	24.0%
7	2.5 to 1	28.0%
8	2.25 to 1	32.0%
9	2 to 1	35.0%
10	1.5 to 1	38.0%
11	1.5 to 1	42.0%
12	1.25 to 1	45.0%
13	1 to 1	48.0%
14	1 to 1	51.0%
15	1 to 1.25	54.0%
16	1 to 1.25	57.0%
17	1 to 1.5	60.0%
18	1 to 1.75	62.0%
19	1 to 1.75	65.0%
20	1 to 2	68.0%

ONE CARD TO COME

OUTS	ODDS	PERCENTAGE
1	45 to 1	2.0%
2	22 to 1	4.0%
3	14 to 1	7.0%
4	11 to 1	9.0%
5	8 to 1	11.0%
6	7 to 1	13.0%
7	6 to 1	15.0%
8	4.75 to 1	17.0%
9	4 to 1	20.0%
10	3.5 to 1	21.0%
11	3.25 to 1	24.0%
12	3 to 1	26.0%
13	2.5 to 1	28.0%
14	2.25 to 1	30.0%
15	2 to 1	33.0%
16	2 to 1	35.0%
17	1.75 to 1	37.0%
18	1.5 to 1	39.0%
19	1.5 to 1	41.0%
20	1.25 to 1	44.0%

GLOSSARY

backdoor: Make a *backdoor hand*. For example, backdoor a flush.

backdoor hand: A hand made in hold'em or Omaha by catching two perfect cards on the turn and river. With a *backdoor flush*, for example, a player starts with two spades and only one comes on the flop. The other two come as the last two cards.

bet for value: Bet a hand with the intention of getting called by one or more lesser hands, as opposed to getting the others to fold. Usually implies betting a hand that has only a slight edge, and one that a conservative player would likely check with. Also *value bet*.

blank: A card on the turn or river likely to be of no help to any player.

button: 1. The disk or other marker that indicates the dealer position in a game dealt by a house dealer. Also known as *dealer button*. **2.** The position from which the dealer would distribute cards if the dealer were one of the players. "I opened the pot, and the button raised."

calling station: A weak player who rarely raises, but calls every bet, even with substandard hands (and hence should not be bluffed).

change gears: Alter the pace of one's playing, usually as a deceptive move against the other players, as, for example, change from fast, aggressive play to a more conservative style.

cufoff: The position to the right of the *button*.

dealer button: See *button*.

limp: Enter a pot by calling the size of the blind, as opposed to coming in for a raise.

flat-call: Only or just call a prior bet, that is, without raising.

flop: 1. As a noun, the first three of the community or board cards. **2.** As a verb, to deal the flop to the center of the table. "The dealer flopped three spades." **3.** As a verb, to make a particular hand or catch a particular card or cards on the flop. "I flopped a flush." "She flopped an ace."

gutshot: An *inside straight* or describing a draw to one.

hole cards: One's starting cards in hold'em; the two private cards dealt to each player.

inside straight: Four cards to a straight with one "hole," as 4-5-7-8 of mixed suits, which becomes a straight by the addition of any 6, or A-2-3-4, which becomes a straight by the addition of any 5, or J-Q-K-A, which becomes a straight by the addition of any 10. (The last two are sometimes called by the special name *one-ended straight.*)

in the hole: Describing one's starting cards in hold'em. "He had A-J in the hole" means his starting cards were and ace and a jack.

in the pocket: Describing hole cards, that is, the two cards a hold'em player starts with. "He had 7-2 in the pocket" means his starting cards were a 7 and a 2.

monster: A big hand for the situation, not necessarily the nuts or even a particularly great hand. Flopping two pair in hold'em against one opponent would be termed a monster by many players.

pocket: Describing hole cards. For example, a *pocket pair* means a player started with a pair and *pocket jacks* means he started with specifically two jacks in the hole.

rainbow: Describing a flop in hold'em of three different suits, usually preceded by the ranks of the cards, as, "the flop came Q-4-3 rainbow."

river: 1. As a noun, the fifth of the community or board cards. **2.** As a verb, to make a particular hand or catch a particular card or cards on the river. "He rivered a flush." "She rivered an ace."

semibluff: Bet with what is currently not the best hand, but with two ways of succeeding. First, your opponent may fold, and you win the pot right there. Second, your hand may improve to a winner. For example, if you bet when all you have is a draw to a straight or flush, and your hand is almost certainly not currently the best, you win if your opponent folds. You also win if your opponent calls and you make the hand on the next card or cards.

slowplay: Not bet or raise with a powerful hand in a normal betting or raising situation, so as to trap other players.

standard deviation: Standard deviation is a concept of statistics. Technically, it's the square root of the variance, which is a measure of the spread of a statistical distribution about its mean or center. Less technically, it's a measure of how far off your hourly expectation is likely to be. We don't need to go into a detailed mathematical explanation, though. In general, the higher your variance, and thus the greater the standard deviation, the larger the bankroll you need.

take a free card: Opt not to bet so one can see the next card without having to put anything into the pot. Often done by a player in last position who has a draw, marginal, or weak hand, and who thinks he might be beat, has been checked to, and thinks he cannot get opponents to fold by betting and that he might get check-raised if he does bet.

the nuts: The best possible hand at the time. For example, if you have K-J and the board reads A♠ Q♠ 10♦ 4♣ 7♥, you have the nuts.

turn: 1. As a noun, the fourth of the community or board cards. **2.** As a verb, to make a particular hand or catch a particular card or cards on the turn. "He turned a flush." "She turned an ace."

value bet: *Bet for value.*

variance: A measure of the spread of a statistical distribution about its mean or center. With respect to poker, the distribution of your results over a set of hands or sessions, or the swings in a positive or negative direction of cash flow. The greater the variance, the wilder the swings; the lower the variance, the more likely a given session results will be close to one's average result. Generally associated with *standard deviation*.

GREAT CARDOZA POKER BOOKS
ADD THESE TO YOUR LIBRARY - ORDER NOW!

CRASH COURSE IN BEATING TEXAS HOLD'EM *by Avery Cardoza.* Perfect for beginning and somewhat experienced players who want to jump right into the action and play cash games, local tournaments, online poker, and the big televised tournaments where millions of dollars can be made. Both limit and no-limit hold'em games are covered, along with the essential strategies needed to play profitably on the pre-flop, flop, turn, and river. The good news is that you don't need to memorize hands or be burdened by math to be a winner—just play by the no-nonsense basic principles outlined in this book. There's a lot of money to be made and Cardoza shows you how to go and get it. 208 pages, $14.95

WINNER'S GUIDE TO TEXAS HOLD'EM POKER *by Ken Warren.* You'll learn how to play every hand from every position with every type of flop. Learn the 14 categories of starting hands, the 10 most common hold'em tells, how to evaluate a game for profit, the value of deception, the art of bluffing, eight secrets to winning, starting hand categories, position, and more! Includes detailed analysis of the top 40 hands and the most complete chapter on hold'em odds in print. Over 400,000 copies sold! 224 pages, $16.95.

HOW TO PLAY WINNING POKER *by Avery Cardoza.* New and completely updated, this classic has sold more than 250,000 copies. Includes major new coverage on playing and winning tournaments, online poker, limit and no-limit hold'em, Omaha games, seven-card stud, and draw poker (including triple draw). Includes 21 essential winning concepts of poker, 15 concepts of bluffing, how to use psychology and body language to get an extra edge, plus information on playing online poker. 256 pages, $14.95.

KEN WARREN TEACHES TEXAS HOLD'EM *by Ken Warren.* This is a step-by-step comprehensive manual for making money at hold'em poker. 42 powerful chapters teach you one lesson at a time. Great practical advice and concepts with examples from actual games and how to apply them to your own play. Lessons include: starting cards, playing position, raising, check-raising, tells, game/seat selection, dominated hands, odds, and much more. This book is already a huge fan favorite and best-seller! 416 pages, $26.95.

OMAHA HIGH-LOW: Play to Win with the Odds *by Bill Boston.* Selecting the right hands to play is the most important decision you'll make in Omaha high-low. More than any other poker game, Omaha is driven by hand value. This is the *only* book that shows you the chances that every one of the 5,278 Omaha high-low hands has of winning the high end of the pot, the low end of it, and how often it is expected to scoop all the chips. You get all the vital tools needed to make critical preflop decisions based on the results of more than 500 million computerized hand simulations. You'll learn the 100 most profitable Omaha high-low starting cards, trap hands to avoid, 49 worst hands, 30 ace-less hands that can be played for profit, and the three bandit cards you must know to avoid unnecessarily losing hands. 248 pages, $19.95.

POKER TALK: Learn How to Talk Poker Like a Pro *by Avery Cardoza.* This fascinating and fabulous collection of colorful poker words, phrases, and poker-speak features more than 2,000 definitions. No longer is it enough to know how to walk the walk in poker, you need to know how to talk the talk! Learn what it means to go all in on a rainbow flop with pocket rockets and get it cracked by cowboys, put a bad beat on a calling station, and go over the top of a producer fishing for a gutshot to win a big dime. You'll soon have those railbirds wondering what *you* are talking about. 304 pages, $9.95.

HOW TO WIN AT OMAHA HIGH-LOW POKER *by Mike Cappelletti.* Clearly written strategies and powerful advice shows the essential winning strategies for beating Omaha high-low poker! This money-making guide includes more than 60 hard-hitting sections on Omaha. Players learn the rules of play, best starting hands, strategies for the flop, turn, and river, how to read the board for both high and low, dangerous draws, and how to beat low-limit tournaments. Includes odds charts, glossary and low-limit tips. 304 pgs, $19.95.

GREAT CARDOZA POKER BOOKS

ADD THESE TO YOUR LIBRARY - ORDER NOW!

I'M ALL IN: High Stakes, Big Business, and the Birth of the World Poker *Tour by Lyle Berman with Marvin Karlins.* Lyle Berman recounts the amazing tale of how he revolutionized and revived the game of poker and transformed America's culture in the process. You'll find this book fascinating, intriguing, and utterly educational, and you'll get the inside story of the man who created the World Poker Tour, You'll read about the exciting and perilous worlds of high-stakes gambling where a million dollars can be won or lost in a single game, and high stakes business where hundreds of millions of dollars can be made or lost on a single deal. Along the way, Lyle reveals 13 secrets of being a successful businessman, the six ways poker players self-destruct, the seven essential principles of winning at poker, and eight steps to a more satisfying life. Savor Lyle's wit and wisdom and learn how to win in business, in poker, and in life. Foreword by Donald Trump. Hardback, photos. 232 pages, $24.95.

POKER WISDOM OF A CHAMPION *by Doyle Brunson.* Learn what it takes to be a great poker player by climbing inside the mind of poker's most famous champion. Fascinating anecdotes and adventures from Doyle's early career playing poker in roadhouses are interspersed with lessons from the champion who has made more money at poker than anyone else in history. Learn what makes a great player tick, how he approaches the game, and receive candid, powerful advice from the legend himself. 192 pages, $14.95.

BOBBY BALDWIN'S WINNING POKER SECRETS *by Mike Caro with Bobby Baldwin.* The fascinating account of 1978 World Champion Bobby Baldwin's early career playing poker in roadhouses and against other poker legends is packed with valuable insights on how he approaches the game. Covers the common mistakes average players make at seven poker variations and the dynamic winning concepts they must employ to win. Endorsed by superstars Doyle Brunson and Amarillo Slim. 208 pages, $14.95.

COWBOYS, GAMBLERS & HUSTLERS: The True Adventures of a Rodeo Champion & Poker Legend *by Byron "Cowboy" Wolford.* Ride along with the road gamblers in the 1960s and feel the fear and frustration of being hijacked, getting arrested for playing poker, and having to outwit card sharps and scam artists. Wolford survived it all to win a WSOP gold bracelet playing with poker greats Amarillo Slim, Johnny Moss, and Bobby Baldwin (and 30 rodeo belt buckles). Read fascinating yarns about life in the rough, including colorful adventures in smoky backrooms with legends Titanic Thompson and Doyle Brunson, and get a look at vintage Las Vegas when Cowboy's friend, Benny Binion, ruled Glitter Gulch. Bobby Baldwin says, "Cowboy is probably the best gambling story teller in the world." 304 pages, $19.95.

SECRETS OF WINNING POKER *by Tex Sheahan.* This new update is expanded to include Tex's other classic work, *Gambling with the Best of 'em.* Long considered one of the must-have books by professionals, this classic contains the timeless winning information every player needs to win money at poker. Sheahan provides sound advice on winning poker strategies for hold'em, 7-card stud, and tournament play, tips on psychology, and personality profiles to go along with some very funny stories from the greenfelt jungle. "Some of the best advice you'll ever read on how to win at poker," says Doyle Brunson. 280 pages, $14.95.

WINNER'S GUIDE TO OMAHA POKER *by Ken Warren.* concise and easy-to-understand, Warren shows beginning and intermediate Omaha players how to win from the first time they play. You'll learn the rules, betting and blind structure, why you should play Omaha, the advantages of Omaha over Texas hold'em, glossary, reading the board, basic strategies, Omaha high, Omaha high-low split 8-or-better, how to play draws and made hands, evaluation of starting hands, counting outs, computing pot odds, the unique characteristics of split-pot games, the best and worst Omaha hands, how to play before the flop, how to play on the flop, how to play on the turn and river, and much more. 224 pages, $19.95

FROM CARDOZA'S EXCITING LIBRARY
ADD THESE TO YOUR COLLECTION - ORDER NOW!

SUPER SYSTEM *by Doyle Brunson.* This classic book is considered by the pros to be the best book ever written on poker! Jam-packed with advanced strategies, theories, tactics and money-making techniques—no serious poker player can afford to be without this hard-hitting information. Includes 50 pages of the most precise poker statistics ever published. Features chapters written by poker's biggest superstars, such as Dave Sklansky, Mike Caro, Chip Reese, Bobby Baldwin, and Doyle—two world champions and three master theorists. Essential strategies, advanced play, and no-nonsense winning advice on making money at 7-card stud (razz, high-low split, cards speak, and declare), draw poker, lowball, and hold'em (limit and no-limit).This is a must-read. 628 pages, $29.95.

SUPER SYSTEM 2 *by Doyle Brunson.* The most anticipated poker book ever, SS2 expands upon the original with more games and professional secrets from the best in the world. Superstar contributors include Daniel Negreanu, winner of multiple WSOP gold bracelets and 2004 Poker Player of the Year; Lyle Berman, three-time WSOP gold bracelet winner, founder of the World Poker Tour, and super-high stakes cash player; Bobby Baldwin, 1978 World Champion; Johnny Chan, two-time World Champion and 10-time WSOP bracelet winner; Mike Caro, poker's greatest researcher, theorist, and instructor; Jennifer Harman, the world's top female player and one of the 10 best overall; Todd Brunson, winner of more than 20 tournaments; and Crandall Addington, no-limit hold'em legend. 672 pgs, $34.95.

CARO'S BOOK OF POKER TELLS *by Mike Caro.* One of the 10 greatest books written on the game of poker, this must-have book should be in every player's library. If you're serious about winning, you'll realize that most of the profit comes from being able to read your opponents. This book reveals the the secrets of interpreting *tells*—physical reactions that reveal information about a player's cards—such as shrugs, sighs, shaky hands, eye contact, and many more. Learn when opponents are bluffing, when they aren't and why—based solely on their mannerisms. Over 170 photos of poker players in action and play-by-play examples show the actual tells. These powerful eye-opening ideas can give you the decisive edge at the table. 320 pages, $24.95.

CARO'S GUIDE TO DOYLE BRUNSON'S SUPER SYSTEM *by Mike Caro.* Working with World Champion Doyle Brunson, the legendary Mike Caro has created a fresh look to the "Bible" of all poker books, adding new and personal insights that help you understand the original work. Caro breaks 36 concepts into the following categories: analysis, commentary, concept, mission, play-by-play, psychology, statistics, story, or strategy. Lots of illustrations and winning concepts give even more value to this great work. 86 pages, 8 1/2 x 11, $19.95.

CARO'S FUNDAMENTAL SECRETS OF WINNING POKER *by Mike Caro.* Learn the essential strategies, concepts, and plays that comprise the very foundation of winning poker play. Learn to win more from weak players, equalize stronger players, bluff a bluffer, win big pots, where to sit against weak players, and the six factors of strategic table image. Includes selected tips on hold'em, 7-card stud, draw, lowball, tournaments, more. 160 pages, 12.95.

7-CARD STUD: The Complete Course in Winning at Medium & Lower Limits *by Roy West.* Learn the latest strategies for winning at $1-$4 spread-limit up to $10-$20 fixed-limit games. Covers starting hands, third to seventh street strategy for playing most hands, overcards, selective aggressiveness, reading hands, secrets of the pros, psychology, and more in a 42 lesson informal format. Includes bonus chapter on 7-stud tournament strategy by World Champion Tom McEvoy. 224 pages, paperback, $19.95.

OMAHA HIGH-LOW POKER *by Shane Smith.* Learn essential winning strategies for beating Omaha high-low; the best starting hands, how to play the flop, turn, and river, how to read the board for both high and low, dangerous draws, and how to win low-limit tournaments. Smith shows the differences between Omaha high-low and hold'em strategies. Includes odds charts, glossary, low-limit tips, and strategic ideas. 84 pages, 8 x 11, spiral, $17.95.

Order now at 1-800-577-WINS or go online to:www.cardozapub.com

THE CHAMPIONSHIP SERIES
POWERFUL BOOKS YOU <u>MUST</u> HAVE

CHAMPIONSHIP HOLD'EM TOURNAMENT HANDS *by T. J. Cloutier & Tom McEvoy*. An absolute must for hold'em tournament players. Two legends show you how to become a winning tournament player at both limit and no-limit hold'em games. Get inside their heads as they think their way through the correct strategy at 57 limit and no-limit starting hands. Cloutier and McEvoy show you how to use skill and intuition to play strategic hands for maximum profit in real tournament scenarios and how 45 key hands were played by champions in turnaround situations at the WSOP. Gain tremendous insights into how tournament poker is played at the highest levels. 368 pages, $29.95.

CHAMPIONSHIP WIN YOUR WAY INTO BIG MONEY HOLD'EM TOURNAMENTS *by Brad Dougherty & Tom McEvoy*. Every year satellite players win their way into the $10,000 WSOP buy-in event and emerge as millionaires or champions. You can too! Learn from two world champions, the specific, proven strategies for winning almost any satellite. Covers the 10 ways to win a seat at the WSOP, how to win limit hold'em and no-limit hold'em satellites, one-table satellites, online satellites, and the final table of super satellites. Includes a special chapter on no-limit hold'em satellites! 320 pages, $29.95.

CHAMPIONSHIP TOURNAMENT POKER *by Tom McEvoy*. Enthusiastically endorsed by more than five world champions, this is a *must* for every player's library. McEvoy lets you in on the secrets he has used to win millions of dollars in tournaments and the insights he has learned competing against the best players in the world. Packed solid with winning strategies for 11 games with extensive discussions of 7-card stud, limit hold'em, pot and no-limit hold'em, Omaha high-low, re-buy, half-and-half tournaments, satellites, and includes strategies for each stage of tournaments. 416 pages, $29.95.

HOW TO WIN NO-LIMIT HOLD'EM TOURNAMENTS *by Tom McEvoy & Don Vines*. Learn the basic concepts of tournament strategy and how to win big by playing small buy-in events, graduate to medium and big buy-in tournaments, adjust for short fields, huge fields, and slow and fast-action events. Plus how to win online no-limit tournaments. You'll also learn how to manage a tournament bankroll and get tips on table demeanor for televised tournaments. See actual hands played by finalists at WSOP and WPT championship tables with card pictures, analysis and useful lessons from the play. 376 pages, $29.95.

POKER TOURNAMENT TIPS FROM THE PROS *by Shane Smith.* Essential advice from poker theorists, authors, and tournament winners on the best strategies for winning the big prizes at low-limit rebuy tournaments. Learn the best strategies for each of the four stages of play—opening, middle, late and final—how to avoid 26 potential traps, advice on rebuys, aggressive play, clock-watching, inside moves, top 20 tips for winning tournaments, and more. Advice from McEvoy, Caro, Malmuth, Ciaffone, others. 160 pages, $19.95.

NO-LIMIT TEXAS HOLD'EM: The New Player's Guide to Winning Poker's Biggest Game *by Brad Daugherty & Tom McEvoy*. For experienced limit players who want to play no-limit or rookies who have never played before, two world champions give readers a crash course in how to join the elite ranks of million-dollar, no-limit hold'em tournament winners and cash game players. You'll learn the four essential winning skills: how to evaluate the strength of a hand, how to determine the amount to bet, how to understand opponents' play, and how to bluff and when to do it. 74 game scenarios and two unique betting charts for tournament play and sections on essential principles and strategies, show you how to get to the winners circle. Special section on beating online tournaments. 288 pages, $24.95.

CARDOZA POKER BOOKS
POWERFUL INFORMATION YOU <u>MUST</u> HAVE

CHAMPIONSHIP NO-LIMIT & POT-LIMIT HOLD'EM *by T. J. Cloutier & Tom McEvoy*. This is the bible of winning pot-limit and no-limit hold'em tournaments. You'll get all the answers here—no holds barred—to your most important questions: How do you get inside your opponents' heads and learn how to beat them at their own game? How can you tell how much to bet, raise, and reraise in no-limit hold'em? When can you bluff? How do you set up your opponents in pot-limit hold'em so that you can win a monster pot? What are the best strategies for winning no-limit and pot-limit tournaments, satellites, and supersatellites? Rock-solid and inspired advice you can bank on from two of the most recognizable figures in poker. 304 pages, $29.95.

CHAMPIONSHIP HOLD'EM *by T. J. Cloutier & Tom McEvoy*. Hard-hitting hold'em the way it's played *today* in both limit cash games and tournaments. Get killer advice on how to win more money in rammin'-jammin' games, kill-pot, jackpot, shorthanded, and full table cash games. You'll learn the thinking process before the flop, and on the flop, turn, and river with specific suggestions for what to do when good or bad things happen. Plus 20 illustrated hands with play-by-play analyses, specific advice for rocks in tight games, weaklings in loose games, experts in solid games, how hand values change in jackpot games, when you should fold, check, raise, reraise, check-raise, slowplay, and bluff. Also tournament strategies for small buy-in, big buy-in, rebuy, add-on, satellite and big-field major tournaments. Wow! If you want to win at limit hold'em, you need this book! 392 pages, $29.95.

CHAMPIONSHIP OMAHA (Omaha High-Low, Pot-limit Omaha, Limit High Omaha) *by Tom McEvoy & T.J. Cloutier*. Clearly-written strategies and powerful advice from Cloutier and McEvoy who have won four World Series of Poker Omaha titles. Powerful advice shows you how to win at low-limit and high-stakes games, how to play against loose and tight opponents, and the differing strategies for rebuy and freezeout tournaments. Learn the best starting hands, when slowplaying a big hand is dangerous, what danglers are and why winners don't play them, why pot-limit Omaha is the only poker game where you sometimes fold the nuts on the flop and are correct in doing so, and, overall, how you can win a lot of money at Omaha! 296 pages, illustrations, $29.95.

CHAMPIONSHIP TABLE (at the World Series of Poker) *by Dana Smith, Ralph Wheeler, & Tom McEvoy*. *Championship Table* celebrates three decades of poker greats who have competed to win poker's most coveted title. This book gives you the names and photographs of all the players who made the final table, pictures the last hand the champion played against the runner-up, how they played their cards, how much they won, plus fascinating interviews and conversations with the champions. This fascinating and invaluable resource book includes tons of vintage photographs. 208 pages, $19.95.

HOW TO WIN THE CHAMPIONSHIP: Hold'em Strategies for the Final Table, *by T.J. Cloutier*. If you're hungry to win a championship, this is the book that will pave the way to success! T.J. Cloutier, the greatest tournament poker player ever—he has won 59 major tournament titles and appeared at 39 final tables at the WSOP, both more than any other player in the history of poker—shows how to get to the final table where the big money is made and then how to win it all. You'll learn how to build up enough chips to make it through the early and middle rounds and then how to employ T.J.'s own strategies to outmaneuver opponents at the final table and win championships. T.J. shows you how to adjust your play depending upon stack sizes, antes and blinds, table position, opponents' styles, and chip counts. You'll also learn the specific strategies needed for full tables and for six-handed, three-handed, and heads-up play. 288 pages, $29.95.

POWERFUL POKER SIMULATIONS

A MUST FOR SERIOUS PLAYERS WITH A COMPUTER!
IBM compatible CD ROM Win 95, 98, 2000, NT, ME, XP

These incredible full color poker simulations are the best method to improve your game. Computer opponents play like real players. All games let you set the limits and rake and have fully programmable players, plus stat tracking, and Hand Analyzer for starting hands. MIke Caro, the world's foremost poker theoretician says, "Amazing... a steal for under $500... get it, it's great." Includes free phone support. "Smart Advisor" gives expert advice for every play!

1. TURBO TEXAS HOLD'EM FOR WINDOWS - $59.95. Choose which players, and how many (2-10) you want to play, create loose/tight games, and control check-raising, bluffing, position, sensitivity to pot odds, and more! Also, instant replay, pop-up odds, Professional Advisor keeps track of play statistics. Free bonus: Hold'em Hand Analyzer analyzes all 169 pocket hands in detail and their win rates under any conditions you set. Caro says this "hold'em software is the most powerful ever created." Great product!

2. TURBO SEVEN-CARD STUD FOR WINDOWS - $59.95. Create any conditions of play; choose number of players (2-8), bet amounts, fixed or spread limit, bring-in method, tight/loose conditions, position, reaction to board, number of dead cards, and stack deck to create special conditions. Features instant replay. Terrific stat reporting includes analysis of starting cards, 3-D bar charts, and graphs. Play interactively and run high speed simulation to test strategies. Hand Analyzer analyzes starting hands in detail. Wow!

3. TURBO OMAHA HIGH-LOW SPLIT FOR WINDOWS - $59.95. Specify any playing conditions, including betting limits, number of raises, blind structures, button position, aggressiveness/passiveness of opponents, number of players (2-10), types of hands dealt, blinds, position, board reaction, and specify flop, turn, and river cards! Choose opponents and use provided point count or create your own. Statistical reporting, instant replay, pop-up odds high speed simulation to test strategies, amazing Hand Analyzer, and much more!

4. TURBO OMAHA HIGH FOR WINDOWS - $59.95. Same features as above, but tailored for Omaha High only. Caro says program is "an electrifying research tool...it can clearly be worth thousands of dollars to any serious player. A must for Omaha High players."

5. TURBO 7 STUD 8 OR BETTER - $59.95. Brand new with all the features you expect from the Wilson Turbo products: the latest artificial intelligence, instant advice and exact odds, play versus 2-7 opponents, enhanced data charts that can be exported or printed, the ability to fold out of turn and immediately go to the next hand, ability to peek at opponent's hand, optional warning mode that warns you if a play disagrees with the advisor, and automatic mode that runs up to 50 tests unattended. Tough computer players vary their styles for a great game.

6. TOURNAMENT TEXAS HOLD'EM - $39.95

Set-up for tournament practice and play, this realistic simulation pits you against celebrity look-alikes. Tons of options let you control tournament size with 10 to 300 entrants, select limits, ante, rake, blind structures, freezeouts, number of rebuys, and competition level of opponents. Pop-up status report shows how you're doing vs. the competition. Save tournaments in progress to play again later. Additional feature allows quick folds on finished hands.